Gone Fishin'...

with

*(How To Take Your Kid Fishing
And Still Be Friends)*

Gone Fishin'...
with

*(How To Take Your Kid Fishing
And Still Be Friends)*

By Joe Perrone, Jr.
and Manny Luftglass

Gone Fishin' Enterprises
PO Box 556, Annandale, New Jersey 08801

Gone Fishin' With Kids
(How To Take Your Kids Fishing And Still Be Friends)
By Joe Perrone, Jr. and Manny Luftglass

Published By
Gone Fishin' Enterprises
PO Box 556, Annandale, New Jersey 08801

ISBN: 0-9650261-4-0
UPC#: 7 93380 12354 1

Photo Credits:
Pictures provided by Al Levey, Marty Marshall, J.B. Kasper, Andy Sharo,
Captain Tom Schafer, Keith Kaufman, Manny's daughter Barb,
and from his private collection, as well as
photos from and illustrations and cartoons by Joe.

Design & Typography:
TeleSet
Somerville, New Jersey

PRINTED IN THE UNITED STATES OF AMERICA

*We dedicate this book, in part, to all those parents
whose intentions were good, but who "screwed it up" anyway;
they were all the inspiration we needed.*

*In addition, I thank my sons: David, Matthew, and Jared,
for "trying" fishing with me,
and I apologize for violating every rule in the book.
I am indebted also to Hans Kooy,
who taught me to love the water;
to Dad in heaven, who bought me my first rod;
to Mom who cooked all those sunnies;
and most of all to my wife, Becky,
for, well, just about everything,
but especially for believing in me and this book.*

Joe

*So now it's my turn.
First, my thanks to my partner Joe,
for asking me to co-author this book with him.
I hate it when someone has a better idea than I do,
but if he ever bugs me about it, I can still blackmail him
about the day we had fishing together at Spruce Run Reservoir.
Next, to my kids, Barb, Sue, Hen & Jen.
I tried to help you enjoy my favorite hobby/sport,
but maybe I tried too hard.
Hopefully, our readers will learn how to do it the right way.
Now, to Barb's Joe, & 'Becca, + Little Hen,
and still more grandchildren to come, —
I promise to do it right this time!*

Manny

Pictured on the cover: *(On the left.)* Seven year old Matthew Levey with a snapper bluefish, caught BEFORE the headboat Pioneer II sailed out of its dock in Jersey City, N.J. *(In the middle.)* "Gramps" Manny with Joseph and Rebecca. Gone Fishin' at a Y Camp Lake in Rhode Island. *(On the right.)* Little Stephanie Marshall was so upset that this largemouth bass had caused brother Martin so much trouble that she was trying to kick it! (Marty released it.)

Pictured on the back cover: *(On the left.)* Here's Norma Lamo, age 8, holding the bluegills she caught at the Clinton Township, N.J.'s P.B.A. Annual Fishing Derby in 1997. *(In the middle.)* See front cover — Gramps did it the right way! *(On the right.)* David Perrone was 9 when he thought that this panfish (chub) was really Moby Dick!

Contents

Introduction

"In the beginning God created the heavens and the earth ..." Then, of course, he made the water and FISH! Ever since then, man has spent an inordinate amount of time trying (mostly unsuccessfully) to catch the critters. AND, for almost as long, he has tried to share his passion for the sport with his offspring with results almost as disastrous.

There were many reasons for writing this book. For example, not one of the children of *one* of the authors fishes — we're not telling you *which* of the authors, but hopefully we can teach *you* not to make the same mistakes he made. In addition, we would like to help you make your particular reason for taking your child fishing work for *you*. Maybe you're only interested in creating another excuse for *you* to go fishing, or perhaps you're hoping to build a better relationship between you and your child. *Whatever* your reason for taking your child fishing, we can both assure you that it is far easier to *screw it up* than it is to succeed!

Sure, we can tell you *how* to do it, *where* to do it, even *when* to do it, but what good is that knowledge if the ones we wish to do it with don't want any part of it?

What can go wrong, and how you can avoid making those fatal mistakes are the *real* reasons we wrote this book. After all, how could *one* of us who had so much to share, screw up so badly? How could *he* have alienated his own kids when all *he* wanted to do was share his time and favorite hobby with his offspring?

Before you go jumping to conclusions, let us say this — perhaps nothing *he* could have done would have changed the outcome with his *own* children, but, we think we've done a pretty thorough job of exploring the mistakes *he* and others like him have made, and we're eager to share our knowledge with you.

Jack Fallon, in his article, entitled "Fishing With Children," published in the March, 1990 edition of *Field and Stream*, wrote "...If you try to mix serious fishing and fishing with children, you and your child will wind up miserable." Think about that. YOU may be very serious about catching Moby Dick, but your kid only wants to be with you, and, *maybe* catch a fish or two. That is the central theme of this book.

Remember, not every young person has to be a Little League star, an Olympian, or a prize-winning BassMasters champion for you to be happy with him. Nor should you *demand* such accomplishments from your child. The strong bonds between adult and child need not be achieved with such pressure, but can be gained through the low-keyed activity of fishing. The same parent who yells at a child for dropping a football pass, muffing a ground ball, or falling on the ice while attempting a triple *whatchamacallit* will probably also be the same parent who scolds his child for losing a fish! If you are that parent, perhaps fishing with your youngster is *not* the thing to do. BUT, if you wish *not* to be that parent, read on and profit from our experience.

In addition to helping you get it *right* where we got it wrong, there'll be lots of "how to" — simplified, of course — as we walk you through the dips and curves along the wet and wonderful road to the world of fishing. Just because you're a beginner doesn't mean you have to wear a sticker on your forehead that labels you as one! We'll introduce you to basic terminology and explore the various types of fishing available where you might live. Don't get nervous though, we promise to adhere to the old principle of *K.I.S.S. (Keep It Simple, Stupid)*.

Okay, now that we've told you what this book *is*, let us tell you what it is *not!* GONE FISHIN' *With Kids* is *not* a be-all, end-all manual detailing the do's and don'ts of child rearing. Neither is it the "COMPLEAT WORLD BOOK ENCYCLOPEDIA OF FISH-

Photo by J.B. Kasper

Kids who fish don't do drugs. To prove it, here's a bunch of them on board the "Big Mohawk," Belmar, N.J.

ING", filled with "over 10,000 full-color illustrations!" It's simply a book to teach you how to take a kid fishing — nothing more, nothing less.

Think you're ready to get started? Then let's GO' FISHIN' *With Kids!*

CHAPTER 1

Why Take A Kid Fishing?

D espite what you might think, there is only one reason to take a kid fishing. That's it — just ONE! But, it's the ONE and ONLY reason that will virtually GUARANTEE success — and that reason can be summed up in just one word — FUN! Sound simple? It is! And, therein lies the secret to making fishing something that you and your child can share for the rest of your lives.

Oh sure, there are love, companionship, good health, food on the table, and a zillion other reasons to take a kid fishing, but if you're not out to have a good time with your child then you are doomed to failure before you even start.

Grown men have been fishing since the beginning of time; and for a variety of reasons. Originally it probably began with cavemen trying to fill the bellies of their families. Then, perhaps, it became a way for henpecked husbands to *get away* from their wives! Maybe, then, it became a way to get together with their girl friends. Then, who knows, perhaps it became a vehicle to get away with one's best friend. But, one thing is for certain; those adults who *continued* to fish did so for the best reason of all — the ONLY true reason — to have fun!

NOTE: *In the January, 1989 edition of* Boating Magazine, *there's an article, labeled "Child's Play," written by Jan Fogt. Two different messages scream out from this story: the first is the sub-title, "Keep it Fun When Teaching Kids to Fish!;" and "It's also important to plan a fishing trip around calm water, because you don't want to take a kid out and beat him up in rough water!"*

WOW! doesn't this sound like great advice? (We will expand upon the latter concept in Chapter 2: Where Do We Go?)

Think about what it means to be a kid. Being a kid is all about HAVING FUN! Hell, that's how most of us can tell when we've become adults — we *stop* having fun. It's true! AND, if we *are* having fun, what's the first thing some wise adult will say? YOU'RE ACTING JUST LIKE A KID! Well, we don't know about you, but there must be a fate worse than being called a kid. Call it the Peter Pan syndrome, but each of us wants to live forever and, yes, each of us wants to have as much FUN as possible.

WHAT'S THE RIGHT AGE
AND WHEN SHOULD WE GO?

If you're old enough to have a child, you're old enough to fish. OH! You were talking about your *child!* Well, since most schools have determined that the age of five years is appropriate for structured learning to begin, we could probably agree upon that age as the proper time. *Except* that many of us know of five-year olds who can't even suck their own thumbs at that age, let alone fish. Still others are capable of playing Beethoven's "Moonlight Sonata" at the ripe old age of five. Which child is yours? Only you can say. Suffice it to say that in order to fish, a child ought to have a reasonable attention span, and coordination enough to tie his or her own shoelaces. The important thing is that a youngster should be *curious* about fishing and display a *genuine interest* in sharing your pastime. If that curiosity and interest is present, then the chances are good that your child is the right age.

The answer to the second part of the question listed at the beginning of this section should be easy — you go fishing when the weather is perfect and you have lots of spare time, right? Wrong! Well, not quite. In *reality,* it's not always that simple. THE BEST TIME TO GO FISHING IS WHEN YOUR CHILD WANTS TO GO! GOT IT? Let us repeat that. THE BEST TIME TO GO

"HEY, DAD! ARE YOU UP YET?"

FISHING IS WHEN YOUR CHILD WANTS TO GO! Having said that, *don't* take your youngster fishing in a thunderstorm, or when the ambient temperature is minus 10 degrees Fahrenheit. Oh sure, you'll eliminate the need for radical rain gear if you adhere to this advice, but don't let the threat of a little shower deter you either, since a little unfettered enthusiasm on the part of a youngster can go a long way toward minimizing the effects of a bit of light rain.

If you can't manage an all-day affair, that's okay, too. In fact, with MOST really young kids, you probably won't want to. Just make it half a day, or even HALF AN HOUR! But, remember, the time to go fishing is when your child *wants to go!*

A WARNING

If you are already an avid fisherman, BEWARE, because YOU have the best chance of screwing up this whole deal! That's right, those of us who really love fishing, face the biggest challenge of all, because *we* are bound to get wrapped up in the *details* of fishing and lose sight of our *objective,* that being to have FUN with our child. Remember, the parent who yells at his child for losing a fish is probably the same idiot who whacks his kid in the back of the head for dropping a pass in the end zone. DON'T BE THAT GUY!

It's quite simple, really. You see, in the first place, our child is with us because he or she WANTS to be. They *like* us. Don't mess with that! Catching a fish is just icing on the cake as far as they are concerned. THEY'RE KIDS, remember? They're not trying to escape from the pressures of the job, or the wife, or the bills; they just want to be with dad and have FUN.

The same father who buys his kid a complete set of S & K auto wrenches when he's three years old will be the one to outfit his youngster with a thousand-dollar rod and reel combo before the kid can even *say* fish, much less understand *what* one is. DON'T DO IT!

So...you've been warned!

OTHER BENEFITS

NOW, for the good part! Let's assume that you've taken up the Holy Grail; you understand *why* you and your kid are going fishing and you've resigned yourself to having fun. What else can you reasonably expect from this "fishing thing?" Well, for starters, there's the *health* bit." What?" you say. "I thought you said ... Relax!" We said your MAIN objective was to have FUN — we didn't say there couldn't be other benefits. GOTCHA!

FIRST comes the FUN, then comes the bonding, companionship, the interest in the equipment, planning trips, etc. Go fishing with your son or daughter for the pure joy of being together and having a really great time — the rest will follow. As your child grows older, you can get more technical — even enjoy a level of competition. AND, eventually have a source from whom to borrow some really *good* equipment! But, that's another chapter ...

CHAPTER 2

Where Do We Go?

P ut simply, you fish where there's water. No, dummy, you can't fish in a drainage ditch, although we can both share a story or two of a nice trout we caught in just such a place, but that's another story.

While there are four basic categories of waters to fish: lakes and ponds; streams and rivers; saltwater rivers and bays; and lastly, oceans; by far the best place to take a youngster fishing, especially for that initial excursion into the piscatorial jungle, is a small lake or pond.

THE FIRST TIME (LAKES AND PONDS)

Be sure the place you choose contains plenty of fish (the variety is not necessarily important, but the *quantity* is!).

Every town has a small lake or pond. Usually the obliging body of water will have a name like "McGee's Pond" or "Old Man Thompson's Lake" or some such imaginative appellation. Just ask at the local bait shop and the gap-toothed clerk will be able to direct you to fish heaven.

The reason we recommend a small lake or pond is simple — the water stands still! You won't have to worry about currents or tides or any other complications which could throw a monkey wrench into your day. Also, lakes and ponds can be fished easily from either the shore or a dock, thereby eliminating the need for a boat which would only serve to complicate matters. Let's face it, a five-year old holding a rod and reel for the first time doesn't

Five year old Samantha DeCleene was not happy holding this pond-caught crappie (calico bass).

need anything confusing like a current or tide to deal with; just trying not to drop the whole outfit in the drink is sufficient challenge for most youngsters the first time out.

Moving water and little kids don't mix. We repeat, *make sure the water doesn't move!* We've all seen regiments of "Miller Men" on Opening Day of trout season drag bleary-eyed contingents of kids to the local stream, only to have their offspring frustrated by currents which not only snag their lines around underwater obstacles, but also carry their favorite baseball caps down to the sea.

Having mentioned "Opening Day," let us say one thing — AVOID 'OPENING DAY' LIKE THE PROVERBIAL PLAGUE! There's nothing worse than throwing a kid into that wild scene where grown men suffering from "cabin fever" act like idiots from a National Lampoon movie. If you've never witnessed such an event, it goes something like this. At precisely eight a.m. (or at whatever time the state authorities have deemed appropriate for the "games" to begin) some idiot wearing a "Smoky the Bear" hat will blow a whistle and hundreds of caffeine-fueled barbarians will rush simultaneously for the same spot on the river. Foul language and even occasional fist fights are the rule, and it's not unusual to see grown men reduced to tears when another fisherman beats them to their favorite spot. Enough said?

Take your child to a small lake or pond the first time around and you'll be rewarded with an experience mutually pleasant to both of you. We promise.

NOTE FROM MANNY: *"I clearly remember the very first day that I took my eldest daughter, Barbara, out fishing. We fished in Prospect Park Lake in Brooklyn on September 4, 1963. It was the day her sister, Susie (don't tell Susie I called her that — I am only allowed to call her Sue) was born. We caught a bunch of golden shiners, and she didn't even get a bellyache from all the junk food I bought her. Truthfully, it was more dumb luck than anything else that made the day a success. I guess I just put the right ingredients together, but to this day, Barb likes to fish more than any of my other three kids."*

STREAMS AND RIVERS

As mentioned earlier, water with current is much more difficult to fish than that which stands still. It is not a good idea to take a beginner to moving water, because even a novice adult usually has no idea how to handle a line in such a situation. If the grown-up is in the dark, imagine how lost the wee one will be.

There is nothing wrong with taking a kid to a stream or river for *practice* — you know, just to get the feel of current and movement. But, do not ever take a child fishing in moving water if it's his or her initial attempt at fishing. Wait until they've been fishing a half dozen or more times before you challenge the current.

Always choose a river or stream that is easy to fish. By that we mean pick one that has open areas along the banks where casting won't be inhibited. Also, try to pick a body of water that isn't full of snags that can catch the youngster's line. Every town with

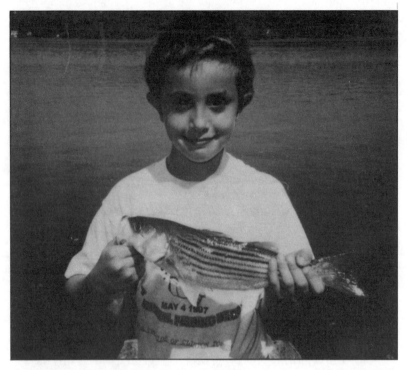

Eight year old Joseph Morea caught and released this small striped bass back into the Thames River in Connecticut.

a river or stream has such a section of water that's easily accessible to fishermen — in fact that's usually where you'll find other youngsters gathered to fish.

SALTWATER RIVERS AND BAYS

There are many fine bodies of water which fall into this category; unfortunately, none of them are found anywhere except on either coast. So, if you live in the interior of the United States, you can forget about saltwater rivers and bays. Needless to say, if you are a thousand miles away from salt (other than that big pond in Utah!) you won't have much interest in ocean fishing either. Although, actually some aspects of ocean fishing can be applied to fishing in large freshwater lakes like those five big ones at the top of the U.S. map. Along the same line, substitute the Mississippi or Missouri River for a saltwater river and you have the same scenario. Basic fishing techniques are adaptable to many different venues.

While we still recommend smaller bodies of still water for the initial fishing experience, saltwater rivers and bays can provide excellent learning grounds for youngsters, if need be, since these places are usually chock full of all kinds of small, easily-caught fish.

Here in the Metropolitan New York area, where we reside, we have several such areas to fish, such as Peconic Bay, the Raritan Bay, the Manasquan River, the Shark River, and other such bodies of saltwater.

OCEANS

If you've never fished in either ocean, let us make you aware of one fact. You can *always* catch *something* in the ocean! We repeat, YOU CAN ALWAYS CATCH SOMETHING IN THE OCEAN! Ergo, oceans are great places to take small kids fishing, right? Wel-l-l-l, maybe. You see, when you fish in oceans, you generally fish on boats. AND, when you fish on boats, there's always the ride out and the ride back — and there are waves, and wind, AND the possibility of SEA SICKNESS! Whoops, you get the picture? So, think twice before you plan an ocean trip. Make sure you go when the weather is guaranteed to be calm and be sure that the first trip is a SHORT one. Let's say an hour or two at the very most. There's no point in scheduling EIGHT HOURS of Hell when one or two will fill the bill!

But, seriously, a brief trip on a calm sea, fishing for a willing species, is a fine way to introduce a youngster to the joys of angling. Just be sure to not violate the basic do's and don'ts and everything will be fine.

FACT: Lake Ontario is an ocean. That's right! Any piece of water where one can only see *more water* in any direction (even with the aid of binoculars) qualifies as an ocean in our book. So, even if you live half a continent away from the sea, don't skip this section on ocean fishing as long as you have Lake Mead, or one of the Great Lakes in your back yard.

NOTE FROM MANNY: *"I took my daughter, Sue (shhh — I still call her Susie when she is not listening carefully) out one day on a half-day drift boat, out of Belmar, New Jersey. The day was not good. Truthfully, it stunk. Cold? Hoo, yeah. Was the wind blowing lightly from the west, causing a pleasant drift on a calm sea? Maybe not. More like cranking from the east, with, urph, five foot seas creating a bucking bronco to ride. Worst of all was when Sue hooked a huge fluke, and it grows each time we talk about it — started at about five or six pounds, but is now up to halibut size. She did everything right and the big shot decided that he needed no help. I grabbed the net, the ten thousand pound net when its mouth was in the water, and I tried to stick it under the struggling flattie. Well, I hit the fish with the side of the net and off it went, in a heartbeat, and Susie ('scuze me, SUE) was talking to the porcelain fixture in the ladies' room for the rest of the outing....she will never forget it."*

A WORD ABOUT BOATS

If you really know what you are doing, and either own a small boat or have access to rental boats, by all means take your youngster out on the water. This can be a wonderful experience, especially since, unlike on a party boat, you can end the day at your convenience, without asking the permission of the captain — try and get it! If your little one tires or simply hates the whole thing, just go on back to the barn and try it another day.

Assuming you have a large pile of money, a super way to start is by chartering a boat. Generally, private tutoring is available and if the youngster learns nothing else, he'll find out who to come to if he ever needs a buck — ouch! Once again, you'll be able to call the shots. If it's too rough, or if little Tommy has a tummy ache, it's your "show;" just have the captain bring the boat back to the dock.

CHAPTER 3

What Do We Fish For?

B asically, "what" you and your child fish for will depend upon two factors: the *age* and *readiness* of your youngster, and *where* you live and what access you have to certain bodies of water. In addition, you must factor in your *own* experience and expertise. After all, you don't want to be playing "let's catch a whale" when you've never even set foot on the sea. You're the parent, remember?

Never expect your little one to demonstrate the same level of skill that you possess, no matter *how* precocious he or she might be. It ain't gonna happen! In fact, it might be better if you left your "experience" at home along with all your fancy equipment. This is for the kid, okay?

FIRST, WHAT *NOT* TO FISH FOR

You may be tempted to have a try for halibut, ling-cod, or giant salmon off the Alaska coast, but these are not critters for your tyke to tackle. Forget too, the five-day exotic excursions off the California coast, heading down to the Baja Peninsula for albacore and such. Instead of "Battle at Baja" it could turn out to be "Bah-Humbug!" Make the "quest" kiddie-sized, not daddy-sized.

Have you ever ridden a "head" boat out to George's Bank for cod? This a marathon trip that involves 24 to 48 hours to complete, and just the boat ride is enough to make strong men weep. Leave Johnny at the pier!

Want to try the Great Lakes for huge salmon and trout? Might be a terrific idea when your youngster reaches his teens, but not so good for a little one. The lake can become an ocean with tummy-tossing waves, and an experience on the freshwater "salt" could turn your child off to fishing forever. Besides, many an adult angler has trouble with a twenty-plus pound fish; you can be assured that an eight-year old definitely won't be up to the task.

"Okay, okay," to quote actor Joe Pesci in "Lethal Weapon II," so what's left? PLENTY! the man said.

To make things easier, let's break down the acceptable species into freshwater and saltwater.

FRESHWATER

Since everyone has access to *some* freshwater fishery somewhere, we'll start there. If you remember, that's where we urged you to start anyway.

PAN FISH

By far and away the most popular and prevalent of all "pan fish" is the ubiquitous "sunny." This catch-all moniker applies to a variety of small, flat, saucer-sized fish known variously as pumpkin seeds, "brim," bluegills, long-ears, shell crackers, red breasts, etc. Call them what you will, your kid and his friends will surely call them "sunnies" — bet on it!!

These little critters are found in almost every pond in the land, and pound for pound, supply more punch than many so-called "game fish." In addition, they are voracious feeders and will strike at almost anything, including a sloppily-tied knot. Willing quarry, that's what we want!

Other pan fish include yellow and white perch, two species which are also widely distributed throughout the country. They are slender fish with pretty stripes, and kids love to catch them by the bucketful. Yellow perch are also known as "Ned" by some down in the mid-Atlantic states, and often referred to as "Bar perch" in other areas. Call 'em what you want, but, by any name, they are mighty tasty, and you and yours just might want to bring some home for dinner. White perch, too, are found in many states and can often be found in brackish (tidal) water as well as in fresh. Some call white perch "blue nose" because of the tendency that larger ones have to develop a snout that is deep blue in color.

The crappie, also known as calico bass, "strawberry bass," and "speck," is another pan fish that is found in at least half the states in America. Since they tend to "school" (travel in groups), a good catch is a fairly common occurrence, and makes them a worthwhile species for the youngster to pursue.

Rock bass are similar in appearance to calicoes, but are a different fish, and are often found in moving water as well as in lakes and ponds. Spring is a great time to catch a mess of them in the quieter part of a stream. In some parts of the country, these fish are also referred to as "red eyes."

NOTE: *Panfish are referred to in quite a favorable light by author and noted outdoorsman, William G. Tapply in a story he wrote for the June 1992 edition of* Field and Stream. *In the article, entitled, "PANFISH are for KIDS," Tapply says: "Fishing is supposed to be fun, and going after these colorful, easy-to-catch little fighters is your best bet for hooking the first-time angler."*

GAME FISH

A "game fish" is a fish which is pursued primarily for its sporting attributes, e.g. jumping or fighting ability, although many are also excellent table fare, notably trout and salmon. Generally, these types of fish are also more difficult to catch, and require more expertise and technique than a little child usually possesses. However, with a little adult supervision and some good fortune, a few of them just might be caught by your child.

SALMONOIDS

Salmonoids are those fish comprising the salmon and trout families, with the latter being the most frequently sought after by young people in states that feature them in their waters. They are a cold water species and most states have stocking programs

Paladin Charters skipper, Tom Schafer, holding the 12 pound lake trout caught by Andrew Weidl in Lake Ontario, 6/23/96.

which involve placing fish grown in hatcheries into suitable bodies of water.

A good way to get your kid into trout is to frequent a "pay-to-fish" pond. These are located all over the United States. In addition to the fact that you *know* there are trout in the water, most pond operators know that they must keep the perimeter of their oversized puddles clear of weeds and trees, so there'll be NO SNAGS on the back cast! Perfect for *you* as well as your kid. If you have access, try a "pay-to-fish" pond, but be sure to explain the rules to your youngster beforehand so you don't have an unhappy camper. Most places require you to keep everything you catch, and of course to "pay" for the privilege — usually by the pound, or sometimes by the fish. It *can* get expensive! Keep in mind that if you and little Johnny have developed a "catch and release" philosophy, this might not be the place for you.

Salmon, cousins of the trout, are tremendous fighters, but unless you are after the land-locked variety (usually one to five pounds average) or the Kokanee (roughly the same size range) it would be best to leave these species alone until your youngster is in his or her teens. A fully developed Chinook (King) salmon can easily top 30 pounds and could yank the rod and reel out of the hands of an unsuspecting youngster. The same goes for a large Atlantic or Coho (Silver) salmon. BUT, when your kid is ready, a Great Lakes or ocean trip for these species might be quite the adventure.

BASS

This catch-all title applies to many species of fish from largemouth and smallmouth, to white, striped and hybrid (a sterile cross between the male southern white and female striped bass).

By far the most popular, and arguably "America's game fish," is the largemouth bass. This fish is found in nearly all the lower 48 states in one variety or another, and is the fish usually sought after in BassMasters tournaments as seen on T.V.! Although generally caught in the one to five pound range, these frisky fellows can top 20 pounds when found in the waters of Florida, Georgia, Texas and other southern states. Your kid will consistently catch those in the one to two pound class — we promise! You probably will, too! Called "bucket mouths" by some, these fish possess a mouth that's nearly half the size of their body, but, fortunately, they don't have any teeth, and are actually quite docile when landed and held by the lower jaw.

Smallmouth bass are generally smaller than their trophy-sized cousins, but make up for their lack of bulk with a fighting spirit that many consider the best of ALL game fish. These bronze-colored gamesters are usually found in cooler climes and often in rocky-bottomed streams and rivers.

NOTE FROM JOE: *"I once fished a reservoir in northwest Maine called the Dolby Flowage. Some friends and I were*

Joe Morea helped "Gramps" Manny catch this 5 pound hybrid ("Rocket") at Spruce Run Reservoir in New Jersey.

staying at a resort at a nearby lake that proved to be fishless, so, following a tip from some local fishermen, we found our way to this other body of water.

"On my first cast, the plastic worm I was using was swallowed by a four-pound smallmouth, which proceeded to jump three feet in the air about 75 feet directly in front of me. Within five seconds, the fish jumped a second time, this time it was 75 feet to my right! A third jump followed — 50 feet to my left — before I eventually subdued my catch. I had never before caught anything like that 'smallie,' and haven't since."

White bass have a wide range and are willing feeders, in addition to being spectacular fighters. Once again, they are relatively easy to catch and tend to school up, usually assuring a good-sized catch.

The Hybrid or "Whiper" as it is often referred to, is a fish of another color. Also affectionately called "rocket" (by Manny), these strong game fish fight as if they had a "lit one" up their keesters! Great sport!

PIKE

Pike are called game fish by many, and include northerns, muskellunge, walleye, and tigers (another crossbreed). Be sure to keep your little ones away from these critters, sometimes referred to as "snake" by those who fish for them. They are fierce looking and come armed with an impressive set of dentures, quite capable of tearing up the hand of a fifty-year old, let alone a five-year old. The chain pickerel is a smaller second-cousin which can provide good sport, providing it, too, is handled with care. But, in general, it should be LATER for this family of freshwater barracudas!

TRASH FISH

We know, we know — what a *terrible* name for our piscatorial friends. However, since we didn't coin the phrase, we're not going to apologize for it, but tell you simply that this is a category that broadly encompasses fish found in questionable waters (read: polluted) and possessing minimal eating and fighting characteristics — DEPENDING, OF COURSE, UPON WHOM YOU ASK!!

Although carp are included under this heading, there is actually a club in America called "The Carp Anglers Group" which holds fish-ins all over the country to fish specifically for "Mr. Man," as he is sometimes affectionately called. This large-scaled bottom feeder is found in many a pond and lake, as well as in rivers, but be warned, a ten-pounder is not something a tyke is capable of landing.

Although fishing for eels and catfish is enjoyed by many, it is not a pursuit we would particularly recommend for the young beginner. Catfish come equipped with venomous spines which can inflict a painful sting, not to mention the infection that generally accompanies the typical wound. It's true, however, that they do make exceptional table fare (there are catfish farms which specialize in raising catfish for consumption), fight well, and aren't too difficult to catch. If you do decide to take them on, be sure that *you* are the one who handles them, and NOT YOUR KID! Eels are slimy, snake-like critters that are ugly and possessed of a slime layer that resembles something left behind by a slug.

NOTE FROM JOE: *"When I moved to rural New Jersey from Brooklyn at the age of ten, my only fishing experience involved having once dunked a dough ball in the lake at Prospect Park. My father was not a fisherman, but he was an observant parent! He noticed the gleam in my young eyes every time we passed anyone fishing, and the first chance he got, he bought me an inexpensive spinning outfit. I can still remember the reel (it came from Davega Sports, a now-defunct store in the city). It was gold and black and was called a Thunderbird: it even had a picture of that ancient Aztec bird embossed on its side. I only mention the details to emphasize how impressionable young children are and what a mark this early acquisition made upon me.*

"Fortunately, we lived less than three blocks from a local hot spot, and I fell in with a group of boys who fished there regularly. With a little practice, I was soon catching lots of sunnies and perch. One day, however, instead of the usual perch, I caught an eel. This wasn't just your usual eel with two e's, it was an e-e-e-e-e-l! Yes, I had caught the mother of all eels, the 'Grand Mahatmah.' Within seconds, the 'Creature from the Black Lagoon' had somehow wrapped itself around my line and appeared to be working its way up the monofilament towards ME! With a blood-curdling scream, I flung the entire outfit, eel and all, into the murky waters of the now infamous Hackensack River.

"That was the end of that! No more rod and reel, no more fishing, no more perch and sunfish for dinner. I didn't fish again until I was 25 years old! Swear to God!"

So, the lesson is quite simple, if you don't like slimy, snake-like critters, it's a sure bet that your kid won't either! Leave the eels to 80-year old Italian men in sleeveless tee shirts; they appear to be the only ones who enthusiastically catch 'em, smoke 'em, and, yuk, eat 'em! (Note from Joe: if you happen to be an 80-year old Italian man, no offense intended 'cause I'm a 50-year old Italian man.)

Suckers, chub, a.k.a. fallfish and shiners, and the like are not bad to fish for, but few anglers actually pursue them specifically. However, in cold water, they can be fun for a kid to catch, and *may* be the only game in town. In addition, since they are a cinch to catch, they make *perfect* sport for the little fisherman in your life.

SALTWATER

Since many of you aren't near the sea, we'll be somewhat brief in this section. For starters, let's eliminate a few distinct species like cod, halibut, grouper, tuna, sailfish, marlin, and the like, when considering what to fish for in the brine. Catching these deep water fish generally involves a major boat ride — not a good idea for youngsters — not to mention considerable expense. Additionally, these fish are tackle busters, and even if your kid hooks one, it's doubtful he or she will be able to even come close to landing it. For our purposes, we'll stick to inshore fishing, which is generally considered to be any saltwater angling which is done within sight of land.

FLOUNDER

Probably the most sought-after fish in the northern brine are the flounder. They are delicious eating, and, since they don't generally grow too large, make excellent sport for the little anglers. "Flatties" are also finicky feeders with a delicate bite, and youngsters, because of their keen sense of touch, are particularly adept at detecting their fine strikes. In short, "short pants" often make terrific flounder fishermen!

FLUKE

The fluke, often confused with the flounder, is almost identical to its nearby relative, with one notable exception — TEETH! It's got a mouthful! Sounds easy enough, right? Wrong! It gets further complicated below the south Jersey coastline where fluke are also called "summer flounder." To make matters worse, one species features its two eyes on one side of its flat body, while the other has its eyes on the opposite side. Simple test? Stick a finger in its mouth; if it comes out bloody, it's a fluke!

BLUEFISH

The bluefish is another popular species found up and down the east coast. They vary in size from eight to ten-inch "snappers" all the way up to 20-pound bruisers. Aggressive in their feeding habits (they'll devour almost anything) these fish are ferocious fighters, generally travel in schools, and feature a most formidable set of dentures, making them quite capable of removing a finger with ease. While bigger blues are usually caught from boats, the smaller "snappers" are often found around bay-side docks and make great sport for your little one. Skip the ocean party boat trips specializing in blue fishing until your kid is near his or her teens. Sea sickness, blood and guts, boredom — you

*Here's Joe Morea again,
holding the 10 pound striper
"Gramps" caught on the Connecticut-
based headboat, "Hel-Cat."*

name it — and you can often find it on a "head" boat. Trust us on this one. Later on, fine!

PORGIES, GRUNT, ETC.

Other "safe" species that will test you and your little one are porgies, yellowtail, grunt, ling, and mackerel. These are all small fish, present no danger, and are readily caught and landed. Although we've only touched upon the more popular saltwater species, be assured that there are plenty of others to fish for, depending upon where you live.

Keep your saltwater boat trips down to a modest distance, and be sure to get good, accurate weather reports. On the west coast, watch out for west winds which can churn up big waves; on the east side of the states, steer clear of "easterlies" for the same reason. Otherwise, you and your little one might be calling for "Ralph!"

CHAPTER 4

Tackle

Thischapter is not intended to plug products for any particular manufacturers, so don't look for brand names or specific makes or models. Rather, it is intended to give you a general guideline to types of tackle and various equipment particularly well-suited for your youngster's age and ability.

It is not our intention to introduce you to all the superduper, latest craze, top-of-the-line equipment that you "just gotta have — as advertised on T.V." We'll leave that to the cable television shows with names like "Homer's Hot Spot" or "Bill's Fish Factory." We're also not interested in helping you turn your kid into the next BassMasters' champion. Such endeavors bore us both to tears, and frankly, neither of us cares a wit about such competitive fishing. We are more interested in a Boy or Girl Scout outing, entry in a party boat pool, or trying for first prize at the local P.B.A. picnic.

As you will note, one of us is an expert fly fisherman, licensed guide and instructor on some of the most famous trout streams in New York's Catskill mountains. But, you'll not find us instructing you as to which exotic split-bamboo rod you should buy, nor will you learn what feathery creation you should tie onto your natural gut leader. There are plenty of tomes on the art of fly fishing and you'll have to glean your knowledge from their pages.

What we would like to discuss is not what tackle you, the adult, ought to be using, but rather what to get for your child. For our purposes we'll break it down into two categories: tackle for those youngsters under four feet tall, and gear for those over four feet in height.

UNDER FOUR FEET TALL

RODS — Far and away the best rod you can buy for the beginning angler is an old-fashioned cane pole. Choose a long, light, skinny, one-piece job. They're not always easy to find, however, but if you can locate one, it is definitely the way to go. Second best, and much easier to find, is the multiple-piece cane rod sold by most tackle stores. This is not a rod that you want to be using way out in the ocean, but for small streams, ponds, and even off saltwater piers, it's just fine. Just tie on a length of ten-pound test monofilament to the top of the pole (usually just longer than the pole itself) and you are in business. Always keep some extra line handy, in case you have to cut off the original and replace it. While a fiberglass or graphite rod of equal length would most likely be either too heavy or awkward for most little tykes, the bamboo version with its lighter weight should be adequate.

NOTE: *Peter Wright writes (no pun intended) in the June, 1994 issue of* Motor Boat & Sailing, "Cane poles are best for the smallest anglers."

If you should opt for a more modern rod, e.g. graphite/fiberglass, select one that is five feet in length or shorter, either for fresh or saltwater. A longer instrument will be too heavy and probably too cumbersome, as well.

REELS come in two basic types; open-faced spinning and bait casting (also known as conventional). The former has a fixed spool, while the latter has a revolving spool, and should be avoided at all costs, since it is most likely to cause Junior to throw the "Ole Devil Backlash!" If you've ever had to untangle one of these messes you know why we recommend steering clear of this type of reel. Spinning reels, on the other hand, first gained popularity back in the fifties, and virtually eliminated the problem of backlash for most anglers. Try one of these and we're sure you'll be rewarded with much less trouble with tangles. Whereas a bait casting reel is mounted on top of the rod, a spinning reel is mounted *under* the rod. So often you'll see adults fishing with a spinning outfit with the reel sitting *on top* of the rod, *and* reeling backwards, to boot. Do they know something we don't know? Not hardly — they were probably never taught the correct way to use the reel in the first place.

LEFTY OR RIGHTY?

This brings us to one of the more confusing aspects of selecting a spinning reel for your child, the choice of whether to get a "left-handed" or "right-handed" model. Generally, adults prefer to cast with their dominant hand, and retrieve (turn the handle) with their opposite hand. Therefore, a right-handed model is made to reel with the left hand, while a left-handed model is intended to be reeled with the right hand. While it would seem logical to use this same approach when outfitting a youngster, quite the opposite seems to be the case. Unless your kid is already a Little League switch hitter, trying to teach him to cast with one hand and reel with the other is guaranteed to make him nuts! Most little ones aren't capable of using their weaker hand particularly well, so we suggest that they are better off casting *and* retrieving with the same hand.

If your kid is right-handed, buy him a "lefty" reel, and do just the opposite for your "southpaw." Got it? Okay, let's make it even easier. If your youngster is under ten years of age, just get a reel that can be retrieved with the same hand with which he casts. Oh, one final note — the tackle industry is on your side, because almost all of the spinning reels currently on the market are *convertible!* That is to say that the handle can be moved to either side of the reel. So there! Case closed! Later, as your child becomes more coordinated, you can teach him the correct method. Above all, DO NOT HOCK THE FAMILY JEWELS TO BUY YOUR KID A ROD AND REEL! You *do* get what you pay for, however, but it's not necessary to spend a fortune to get decent equipment. Some features to look for would be an extra spool (to hold more line, just in case you get a *major* tangle — you can substitute the extra spool and untangle the other one when you have spare time) and

Indiana resident, Donavan Martin, was visiting relatives
in Florida, and used a rod provided by the half-day drift boat,
"Blue Heron II," out of Jupiter, Florida, to catch this
6 pound mutton snapper.

a ball bearing or two (instead of bushings) which will make the reel smoother to operate.

While a spinning reel is just fine for freshwater, a child out on the salt in a party boat would be equipped with a conventional reel, preferably spooled with 20-pound monofilament. This type of reel *can* backlash just like its cousin, the bait caster, but with its revolving spool and greater strength, it's just what's needed to handle a heavy sinker or diamond jig.

A THIRD KIND OF REEL does actually exist, and it's commonly referred to as a spin cast reel. Most of us who are over forty probably started our kids with one of these old standby outfits because they were cheap! The standard rig was a white, solid fiberglass rod with a black plastic, space-age looking reel mounted on top. Now they come in a variety of colors, usually emblazoned with a cartoon likeness of some popular character, undoubtedly aimed at attracting youngsters.

Down south, bass fishermen still use a version of this contraption, called a closed-face reel. It has its line completely enclosed within a capsule, and is also mounted on top of the rod handle. But, its main attraction is the true ease of casting it provides. You know, hold the button in, point and cast, releasing the button as you come down from the top. Sounds great in theory, but in practice this reel has several serious drawbacks. First of all, there is a tendency for the line to become tangled beneath the cover or "closed face." Usually this results in more severe tangles, because, unlike the spinning reel, where the line is visible (and tangles are evident at once), the initial tangle with a closed-face reel is hidden from view, and becomes increasingly worse with each successive cast. Secondly, and perhaps of more significance, is the fact that you have no idea how much line remains on the spool. Thirdly, just when your child is becoming used to this type of reel, all of his friends are no doubt moving on to spinning or bait casting reel, and Junior is forced to learn all over again. Trust us on this one, we've both been there! Start the child with a reel that allows him to see the line — one that may be a little tougher to learn to cast initially, but the one they will nearly all wind up using later on, anyway.

TERMINAL TACKLE — Definitely buy your kid his or her own little tackle box. Just imagine the pride of ownership this simple act will engender. The box need not be expensive, but just something with enough trays and compartments to handle the following:

HOOKS — Have an assortment of hooks selected for the type of fishing you intend to do. Most people buy the pre-snelled (with leader attached) variety, usually packaged under various headings in plastic bags. These are fine, but are usually a sign of the novice. Most experienced fishermen prefer to make up their own rigs, especially for fishing in saltwater. A batch of various loose

© 1997 Joe Perrone

"... HEY, DAD, DID YA GET THAT LITTLE TANGLE OUT YET?"

hooks is usually better, especially in freshwater. If you're not sure what type of hook to use, ask the fellow in the tackle shop to help you with a selection. First, though, ask him if he's a fisherman, and hope that the answer is "yes!"

SINKERS — Again, ask the guy at the tackle shop, after first explaining what kind of fishing you'll be doing. The last thing you want to do is embarrass your child by tying on a two-ounce pyramid sinker and having him cast it into a pond filled with sunfish. (Just for the record, a pyramid sinker is shaped just like its namesake and is used for surf fishing in sandy-bottomed areas.) Just be sure to have a good assortment, based on where and for what you're fishing.

FLOATS — Some call it a float, some call it a bobber. Forgive the sexism, but if mommy takes little Jane to the lake, you can bet that daughter will have a red and white, grapefruit-sized bobber on the line; pretty to look at, but not at all what's required. Most will agree that the smallest float that will get the job done is usually best. The same goes for hooks and sinkers. Stick to the fixed type of float, rather than a "slip" bobber, or "slider," commonly used in deep water — and especially preferred down south — unless you really know what you are doing.

MISCELLANEOUS — This should include, but not necessarily be limited to: extra line, barrel and snap swivels, a stringer, a pair of long-nosed pliers, a line clipper, lures, and artificial baits. It can also include a half-finished candy bar (complete with ants), a comic book, or even a jar of bubble mix.

The important thing to remember is that the tackle box belongs to your child, and *everything* in it is HIS!

OVER FOUR FEET TALL

Presumably, if your child is over four feet tall, he or she is also older, more coordinated, and less inhibited than the smaller version about which we've been speaking. With these factors in mind, we make the following recommendations:

ROD AND REEL — Buy the appropriate rod for the job at hand. If it's fishing in a pond, stick with the cane pole, but make it a bigger one. If the child is ready, perhaps choose an inexpensive spinning rod between five and six feet long. Usually one outfit will handle most freshwater situations with some adjustments for line weight, etc. A medium action rod, rated for 6-10 pound test line should be fine.

Naturally, saltwater fishing will dictate the use of heavier tackle, with a conventional rod usually the choice, teamed with a reel of sufficient size and strength to handle the species being sought. In either case, match whatever rod you choose with an appropriate reel and line of proper test to match. Your tackle dealer should be a big help here, and it pays to use the same one, if possible, thereby developing a relationship of trust for the days ahead.

NOTE FROM MANNY: "A surf outfit is a nice thing to give to a child, but kids and sand really create superior messes. For openers, a ten-year old will not stay put — period! They also are superduper good at falling down, and if this is done while holding the surf outfit, it is an absolute guarantee that one, the rod will be broken in the fall, or two, the reel will be buried in sand up to its 'yurnim' (that's deep!). One of the silliest things we see is a grown-up on a party boat, using a ten-foot surf stick. Remember the movie "Dumb and Dumber?" That is what father and son will look like if they are at the rail with matching surf rods. Save the surf rig for a far more experienced and older youngster.

We saw two guys out one day on Spruce Run Reservoir in New Jersey, aboard a little twelve-foot boat. They were each using those extra long and skinny 'noodle' rods that are intended for use for salmon on fast-moving rivers. These rods were longer than the boat! Fortunately, both were adults, but if one was a kid, how impossible that would have been to handle. The two adults didn't do much either. In several hours all we saw was the hooking AND losing of one little puny pike, because the rod was too clumsy to use on a boat."

TERMINAL TACKLE — For the bigger children, again, just scale up. Bigger kids can handle bigger fish and the appropriate tackle that they require. You can probably leave the lures in *their* box, along with everything else that the smaller fry might have in theirs.

Acquiring more and better tackle is a great motivator for teaching children how to save. If little Harry wants a better reel, give him odd jobs around the house to earn the necessary money to make a purchase. Encourage your youngster to save for the hot new lure he saw on television. Not only will this teach him values, but it might make him less of a 'sucker' for those 'gotta have it now' commercials when he becomes an adult. You'll also be teaching him to take better care of equipment, especially since he helped pay for it himself.

Remember, as long as the tackle is appropriate for the type of fishing you are doing, it is sufficient. Keep it simple in the beginning and keep the emphasis on fishing, *not* on the equipment!

ARTIFICIAL LURES

While we both discourage the use of artificial lures for most youngsters under the age of ten, those in double digits will probably be inclined to want to use some of the hot new lures they see on T.V. or in their buddies' tackle boxes. To those of you who are accomplished fishermen, the following will probably be old hat. But, if you *aren't* such an experienced angler, read on as we offer a brief discussion of some of the more common types of lures.

SPINNERS — Perhaps the most widely-used lure in existence is called simply a "spinner". This device is nothing more than a wire shaft with a hook attached to one end, and an eye to the other. Usually the hook is a treble, but with the big move toward "catch and release" fishing, more and more models are becoming available with a single hook, which aids in the easy release of the fish. Along the shaft is a blade which revolves as the "spinner" is pulled through the water. In addition to the blade, sometimes several beads are placed on the shaft for decoration, and possibly to serve as noise-makers to help attract fish. Also, the hook may be disguised with a "tail" usually made of some type of hair, like squirrel tail. These lures come in many sizes, from "OO" (the smallest) all the way up to a size "5," with blades of silver, gold, red & white, black, etc. Without a doubt, this is the easiest AND often one of the most productive lures one can use. Virtually any species of fish can and HAS been caught on a spinner at one time or another.

SURFACE LURES — These are usually bait fish imitations, but often include models which can imitate anything from a frog to a mouse (we've even seen some that are shaped like a miniature can of beer — honest!). They are usually molded out of plastic, although there are still some wooden models on the market (some anglers actually seek out the wooden ones, because they claim they float differently and behave in a more effective manner). Generally fished as an imitation of a wounded minnow or other bait fish, most have a lip in front which contributes to a diving and/or wobbling motion when the lure is moved through the water. They come in an endless variety of colors and shapes and are quite effective when fish are taking bait on the surface. Most have several treble hooks attached to them, and should be used with great care, ESPECIALLY when removing them from a hooked fish. Otherwise, you could become the "hookee" rather than the one who does the hooking! When used in saltwater, these are commonly referred to as plugs.

POPPERS — A variation of the stick bait or plug, poppers have a concave front, which serves to throw out a spray of water, and to make a sizable disturbance when pulled hard through the water. Poppers are great in freshwater for stimulating otherwise sluggish bass and other surface strikers, as well as moving saltwater game fish such as stripers or bluefish. These proven "fish getters" also come in many sizes and shapes, and are used to catch any number of game fish.

CRANK BAITS (Also referred to as STICK BAITS) — This is a name applied to a broad spectrum of lures which are fished beneath the surface. Made to imitate forage fish, crayfish, frogs, etc., these lures come with rattles, lights, even sound. As the name suggests, they are most effective when "cranked" hard through the water. They are particularly good because they can be fished at varying depths, thereby reaching fish that may be suspended over underwater structure or elsewhere in the water column.

JIGS — These are hooks with a molded head, usually of lead, but sometimes of glass or plastic. They are generally "dressed" with a tail of some sort: made either of bucktail or some type of flashy artificial material, which waves and wiggles as the lure is "jigged" up and down in the water. Very often these lures will have an additional dressing of pork rind or other such material

Keith Kaufman, editor of Fisherman Magazine's Mid-Atlantic edition, took this shot of two fluke which hit a bucktail jig. In the photo are Ross Kaufman, Lauren & Jeff Kirchoff, and Cody Kaufman.

attached to the hook to make them more attractive. Experienced bass fishermen refer to this type of set-up as a "jig and pig." Another variation of the traditional jig is the "slow-fall" jig, which has an abundance of wiggly rubber legs attached which slow the descent of the jig and add a tantalizing movement to the lure. Plain buck tail jigs in white and yellow are a traditional lure for fluke, flounder and striped bass in the salt.

PLASTICS — This broad category covers virtually anything made of soft plastic or rubber, from worms and salamanders, to leeches and polywogs. These artificials are most often associated with largemouth bass fishing; although imitation rubber eels can be quite effective when fished around rock jetties when angling for striped bass in the brine. This type of lure probably originated with the old standby, the rubber worm, which is now virtually obsolete, but suffice it to say that no respectable "bassin' man" would be caught dead without a supply of "plastics" in his arsenal. One recent innovation has been that of impregnating these crawly critters with various bait scents, which are then released slowly into the water during fishing. Trust us, they work!

SPINNER BAITS — This is a variation of the traditional spinner that looks like a combination between a spinner and a jig. The blade trails the upper portion of something that resembles a large safety pin (there may even be more than one blade). The lower portion of the "safety pin" usually has what appears to be a jig with rubber legs, hiding a large, single hook. These lures are virtually weedless, and can be fished among all kinds of cover with almost no fear of them becoming snagged. Mostly used for largemouth bass, they can also be killers for other freshwater species, especially pike, pickerel and muskies, when used in enormous sizes.

BUZZ BAITS — Almost identical to spinner baits, except that instead of having a blade, they are equipped with a sort of propeller, which churns up the surface of the water, much like a swimming mouse or other small rodent might do. No one really knows what the fish take them for, but as long as they work, who cares?

SPOONS — Also called wobblers, these are blade-shaped lures with a hook trailing off the end. The name probably originated in early fishing days when someone undoubtedly took an actual eating spoon and crafted a lure from it. Most older anglers probably think automatically of a "Daredvle" (a popular spoon, manufactured by a company called Eppinger) when they think of this type of lure. But, in actuality, there are so many variations of the spoon, that it would be impossible to name them all here. Generally, a spoon will be either silver or gold-colored on one side, and the other side will have some type of pattern on it. The number of patterns is limitless, but some of the more popular ones feature red and white stripes, or red diamonds on a yellow background (commonly referred to as a "five of diamonds"). The latter design is particularly deadly for pike when used in very large sizes. Small spoons are also trolled slowly from canoes for species such as land-locked salmon.

Spoons are also used in saltwater. In the sea, some spoon designs are quite radical, being shaped like eels, small bait fish and other forms of bait. They all have one thing in common, however; they all wobble tantalizingly, and have a distinctive side-to-side motion when actively retrieved. Very large spoons which imitate moss bunker (or Menhaden) are often trolled behind boats at slow speeds to catch striped bass.

DIAMOND JIGS, VIKING JIGS, ETC. — Used mostly in saltwater, these types of "jigs" are made of heavy metal with a chrome finish and come in any number of shapes, from elongated diamonds to "S" — shaped eels. They can be as small as a quarter of an ounce to as heavy as a pound. Some have plastic eel-like tails attached, and some are fished plain. Others have bucktails attached to the treble hook, while still others have reflective tape affixed to their sides to add more sparkle. Many are fished with a traditional jigging motion, which involves lowering them to the bottom and "jigging" or lifting them erratically, up and down. Sometimes, the same lure can be cast far out, allowed to fall to the bottom, and then reeled quickly back on an angle — some call this action "squidding." Other times, they are cast out in the surf and rapidly retrieved in an erratic fashion, often bringing smashing strikes from bluefish and the like. They can be tricky to use in the beginning, but if you get the hang of it, they can be deadly for species like striped bass, fluke, mackerel, and the ubiquitous bluefish. The jumbo-sized ones are used with great success for cod and halibut, both bottom dwellers.

MISCELLANEOUS "STUFF"

Suffice it to say that we probably have left out somebody's favorite "GOTCHA" lure; if we have, we're sorry. You name it, however, and we're sure *somebody* has invented it *and* used it successfully! But, hey, that's what tackle shops and a child's allowance are for! Have fun — experiment!

ONE NOTE: *Be especially mindful when allowing young children to use lures of any kind! Since most artificials are equipped with at least one treble hook, accidents can be potentially quite dangerous. Whenever possible, replace treble hooks with single hooks, and flatten the barbs. You might miss the occasional fish, but at least you or your child won't become a fishing casualty statistic. Also, always wear eye protection of some sort, preferably sunglasses with shatterproof lenses. 'Nuff said?*

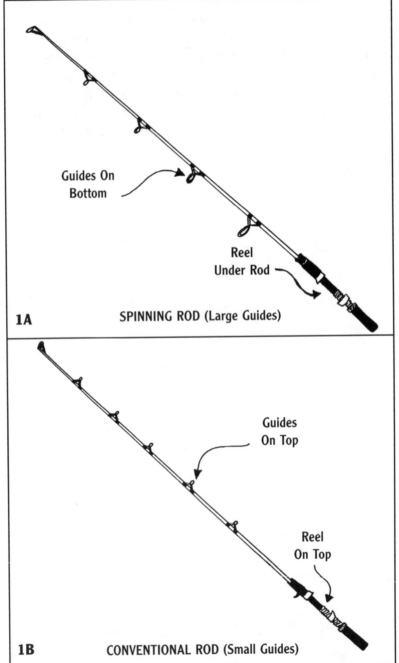

Guides On
Bottom

Reel
Under Rod

1A   **SPINNING ROD (Large Guides)**

Guides
On Top

Reel
On Top

1B   **CONVENTIONAL ROD (Small Guides)**

CHAPTER 5

Some Basic "How To"

As we stated earlier in this book, our objective is to teach you how to take your child fishing with as few complications as possible. With that thought in mind, we offer the following expanded insights into some of the basic terminology, techniques, and skills that will help you do just that.

RODS

There are basically two types of rods: spinning and conventional *(see illustrations 1A and 1B)*. A spinning rod has large guides, designed to allow the line to come off the reel's fixed spool in big coils. The larger guides minimize the friction that would result if the guides were smaller, like those found on a conventional rod. In addition, the reel seat which holds the reel in place is located on the bottom of the rod, just as the guides are. If you are selecting a rod in a sporting goods store, and you are looking for a spinning rod, look for the rods with large guides and you'll be looking at the right ones.

A conventional rod has very small guides, because the line comes off of the revolving spool in a relatively straight line. These rods are used with the guides *and* the reel on top of the rod, and in some models, there will be a trigger type handle to facilitate casting. Whether you choose a one-piece or a two-piece rod is purely a function of space and personal preference. Most fishermen would prefer a one-piece rod, all things being equal, providing that it is convenient for them to travel with it.

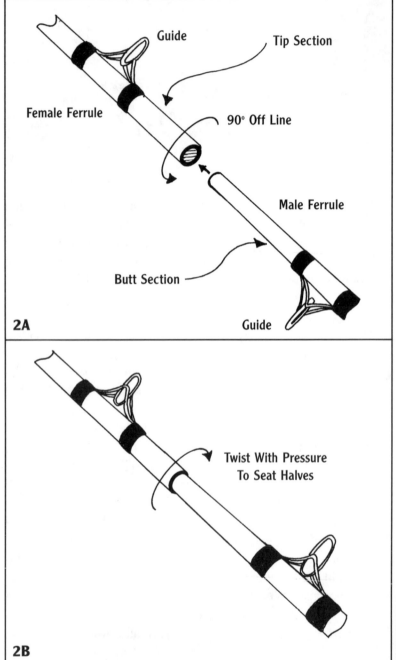

A two-piece rod is made up of a bottom section, called the *butt section,* and a top section, called the *tip section.* The connection between the two sections is made of two parts called *ferrules.* There is a male ferrule and a female ferrule, with the male being located at the tip of the butt section, and the female at the bottom end of the tip section (note: occasionally on some rods, the sequence *may* be reversed). With most of today's rods being constructed of fiberglass, graphite, or a composite of the two, it is imperative that the two sections be connected correctly *(see illustrations 2A and 2B).*

Take the male ferrule of the butt section and insert it into the female ferrule of the tip section, with the guides off line by 90 degrees. Gently press the two sections together until they are relatively snug. Then, using a little pressure, twist the two sections into alignment until they are good and snug! If you don't utilize the twisting motion, your rod may not "seat" properly and might come loose during fishing. When you go to take the rod apart after fishing, pull the two sections from one another with a reverse twist. That's it! *(ONE NOTE: On some older rods, the ferrules are made of metal, usually nickel/silver, and should **not** be twisted. These ferrules **must** be lined up absolutely **straight** and then pressed firmly into position. When taking them apart, they must be pulled **straight** apart, not twisted. Twisting this type of ferrule can result in forcing the ferrule out of round, thereby rendering it useless.)*

SETTING UP YOUR ROD AND REEL

The rod you choose will have either a cork or a synthetic material covering the handle. Either one is fine. The *reel seat* is the device that enables you to mount the reel on the rod, and may take two basic forms. One is a *fixed reel seat (see illustration 3A),* and consists of an insert (usually of graphite, metal, or plastic) which is approximately in the middle of the handle. There will be a recessed hood at the top of the reel seat to accept the top part of the reel foot, and another hood that will slide over the bottom of the foot of the reel. To hold the reel firmly in place, there is a

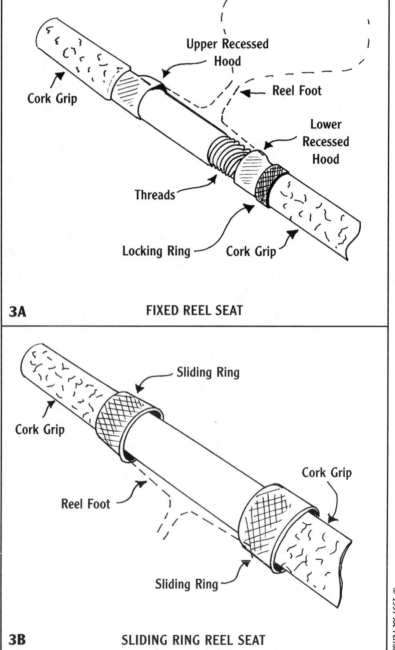

3A   FIXED REEL SEAT

3B   SLIDING RING REEL SEAT

threaded ring that tightens against the bottom hood. Some rods even have an additional ring, called a *locking ring,* which is tightened against the first ring to provide further protection against loosening. Whichever type you purchase, always be sure that you tighten the reel seat as tight as possible. It's no fun to cast your reel into the drink. We've both been there!

On some small spinning rods there are *sliding reel seats (see illustration 3B).* These consist of two sliding rings which are forced over each side of the reel foot and are held in place by friction. They are designed to allow you to move the reel up and down the reel handle to achieve a custom level of balance. We recommend a little electrician's tape, once you have located the reel where you want it to be.

In addition to the two reel seats mentioned above, there is a third possibility which you might encounter. That is the possibility that there will only be a handle and *no* reel seat at all! This type of arrangement is most commonly found on surf rods, and is designed to permit the accurate placement of a reel to allow for the length of a fisherman's arms as well as for the balancing of the overall outfit. Electrician's tape is a must with this type of set up.

Once you have placed the reel on the rod and secured it in place (REMEMBER — SPINNING REEL *BENEATH THE ROD*, CONVENTIONAL REEL *ON TOP*) it is time to line up.

SPINNING OUTFITS

As you will note in *illustration 4A,* a spinning reel has a *bail,* which is a metal half circle containing a *roller guide.* As the handle is turned, the bail revolves around the fixed spool, with the line being held under the roller guide and wrapped around the spool with each turn of the handle. When you first go to line up your outfit, it is necessary to open the bail to allow some line to come off the spool. Be sure to allow enough line off to fully run up through the series of guides and out the tip top of the rod. When you have pulled out enough line, turn the handle of the reel, thereby closing the bail. You will notice that the line will

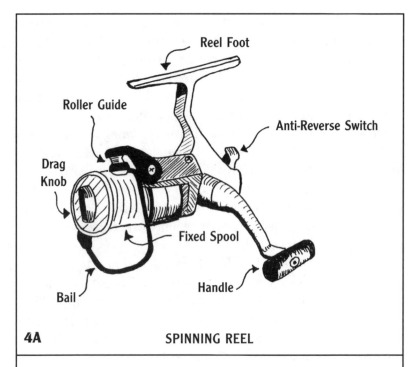

Reel Foot

Roller Guide

Anti-Reverse Switch

Drag
Knob

Fixed Spool

Bail

Handle

4A   **SPINNING REEL**

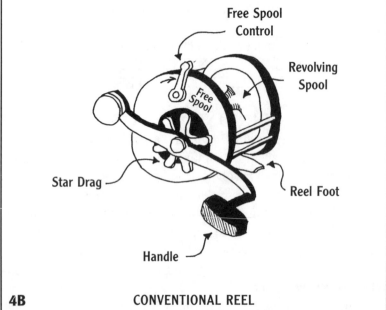

Free Spool
Control

Revolving
Spool

Free
Spool

Star Drag

Reel Foot

Handle

4B   **CONVENTIONAL REEL**

automatically be trapped beneath the roller guide.

Most reels have a switch called an *anti-reverse* switch. With this switch in the *on* position, you will not be able to turn the handle backwards. We recommend always leaving this switch in the *"on"* position. The more you fish, the more self-evident this maxim will appear. Trust us!

CASTING

When you are ready to cast, you hold the rod with two fingers *in front* of the reel and hold the line beneath your index finger, trapping the line beneath your finger and against the handle. Now, open the bail. You will notice that the line is now free to come off of the spool, providing you release it from beneath your finger. Don't release it yet!

Bring the rod back slowly, the same way a baseball pitcher would bring his arm back in order to throw the ball. As you bring the rod forward in a casting motion, release the line from beneath your index finger at the appropriate time necessary to allow your cast to be made to the target. If you release *too soon,* your bait or lure will fly high up into the air. Release *too late,* and your bait or lure will splash directly down into the water in front of you. With a little practice, you'll find the proper release point to allow proper casting direction and distance. WE SAID PRAC-TICE! PRACTICE MAKES PERFECT! BELIEVE IT! You can actually purchase practice plugs made of rubber or plastic *without hooks.* Buy one and take junior to a park and use it until *both of you* can cast like champs. This saves a lot of frustration.

CONVENTIONAL OUTFITS

After securing your conventional reel into the reel seat ON TOP of the rod, loosen the drag adjustment enough to permit you to strip enough line off the spool to reach through the guides and out the tip top. Attach whatever terminal tackle you are going to use, and you are ready to cast. If your reel has a level wind feature, be sure to go through the level wind opening first. Some conventional reels also have a clicker (for fishing with live bait). Be sure that the clicker is also in the *off* position.

A conventional reel has a revolving spool *(see illustration 4B)*, which is mounted laterally, allowing the line to come off with little or no resistance, thereby allowing long, accurate casts when used properly. Having said that, let us caution you against the nemesis of the conventional reel user — BACKLASH! Backlash is what occurs when your lure or bait enters the water upon being cast, *without* the spool ceasing to revolve. Line continues to gush from the reel *without* any weight to pull it away from the reel (remember, your bait or lure is already in the water). The resulting mess is called a "bird's nest," because of its resemblance to its natural counterpart. In order to prevent backlash, it is necessary to develop what is commonly referred to as an "educated thumb."

CASTING

When you cast a conventional reel, you first place the reel into what's known as "free spool." By pushing a button, you allow the spool to revolve freely, thereby allowing line to be pulled from the spool and to be cast. The second you press the free spool button, you must put your thumb upon the spool to prevent it from spinning wildly. You then take the rod back as in a pitching motion and then bring it forward to cast. By releasing the thumb at the proper moment, the lure or bait is cast forward, pulling line off the revolving spool. The trick is to put your thumb *back on the spool* at just the instant that your bait or lure is about to enter the water. If done properly, no "backlash" will occur and everything will be fine.

As in using a spinning reel, if the thumb is released too soon on the cast, the lure or bait will head skyward; too late, and the bait or lure crashes into the water in front of you. Perhaps even more than with a spinning reel, practice with a conventional reel is a *must!* Remember, only with practice will your thumb become "educated!"

DRAG: WHAT IS IT?

We have mentioned "drag" a number of times, and it might

ly a device used to restrict a fish's ability to freely take line from the reel. It also serves another purpose, that being to tire out a fish, so it might be more easily landed. By properly setting the amount of drag (to approximately ¹/₃ the line weight) we also preclude the possibility of line breakage.

A spinning reel usually has a drag adjustment knob located on top of the spool, although, occasionally it might be located at the rear of the reel. By tightening the knob *clockwise,* the amount of drag is *increased.* Conversely, by turning the knob *counter clockwise,* the amount of drag is *lessened.* With practice, you'll develop a feel for the proper drag setting. (There's that word again — practice!)

The drag adjustment on most conventional reels is a "star" shaped affair, located on the same side as the handle. It, too, is turned in a *clockwise* manner to increase drag tension, and *counter clockwise* to lessen drag.

As a general rule of thumb, a proper drag setting allows the fish to take line a little at a time, only when it makes a good, hard pull. If the fish can't take line, then, quite simply, the line will break! Or, perhaps the rod will break! Or you will lose the fish!

"HOOK, LINE AND SINKER ..."

Okay, now you've got your line through the guides, and you know how to cast. What about a knot to tie on your lure or hook?

For the beginning fisherman (that's you, in case you forgot), there is really only one knot that you must learn: the *improved clinch knot.* To tie this knot, it is first necessary to learn a little knot terminology. The end of the line is called the *tag.* The portion of the line behind the tag is called the *standing line.* That's all you need to know. Now, here's how to tie the *improved clinch knot:*

Step 1. Put the *tag end* of the line through the eye of the hook or lure you are intending to use.

Step 2. Take the *tag end* and make five (5) wraps with it around the *standing line (see illustration 5A).*

Step 3. Insert the *tag end* into the first loop above the eye

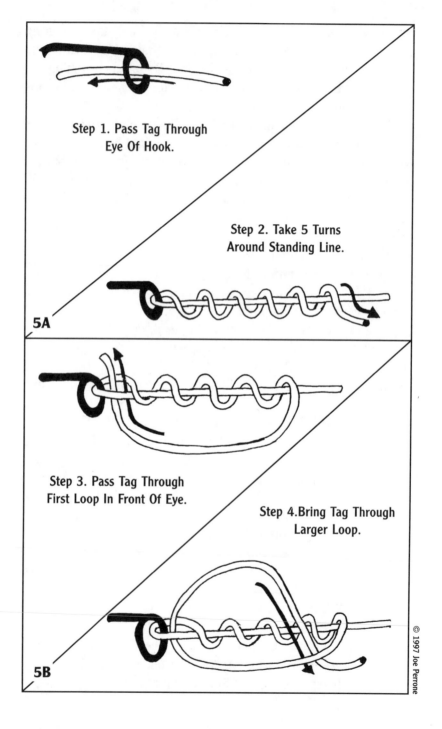

Step 1. Pass Tag Through
Eye Of Hook.

Step 2. Take 5 Turns
Around Standing Line.

5A

Step 3. Pass Tag Through
First Loop In Front Of Eye.

Step 4.Bring Tag Through
Larger Loop.

5B

© 1997 Joe Perrone

(see illustration 5B). In the process of doing this, you will form a larger loop.

Step 4. Bring the *tag end* through the larger loop (this is the "improved" portion of the knot) and tighten by pulling on the *standing line* (be sure to moisten the knot *before* pulling the knot tight.) USE A SLOW, STEADY PULLING MOTION WHEN TIGHTEN-ING THE KNOT. *NEVER* JERK THE KNOT TIGHT. THIS CAN WEAKEN THE KNOT SUB-STANTIALLY.

The *improved clinch knot* will be perfectly adequate for most fishing situations, and certainly for those that a beginner will encounter. Naturally, as you become more experienced and enter into more specialized fishing, the need will arise for specialized knots. In that case it would be wise to invest in a good book on the subject. One which we recommend is *Bob McNally's Complete Book of Fishermen's Knots, Fishing Rigs, And How To Use Them,* published by McNally Outdoor Publications, 1716 Bayside Boulevard, Jacksonville, Florida 32259.

Okay, so now you know the knot, but what do you tie it to? Well, if you are using bait, you'll need a hook!

Since we promised to adhere to the KISS Rule (Keep It Simple, Stupid) let's just say that there's a hook to match every possible species of fish and every type of bait. However, the most common type of hook (and probably the one you'll use most) is call a *bait holder!* Tough stuff, huh? This type of hook has what's called a *sliced shank,* that is the shank has several cuts in it, which results in barbs, which help hold bait onto the hook.

NOTE: *When fishing with youngsters under the age of 10, it is a good idea to pinch down the barb of the hook to avoid accidental injury. It is much easier to remove a hook from a small one's finger, or, for that matter, from a fish, with the hook barb pinched down.*

Once again, keep in mind that your local tackle shop can advise you on the exact type of hook required for your particular kind of fishing. Right now, stick with a basic bait holder and you'll be fine.

WHAT SIZE HOOK?

Before we get involved with hook size, let's talk about *how* hooks are sized! Hooks used for freshwater fishing are sized from #1 all the way down to #32 (used in fly fishing). The *higher* the number of the hook, the *smaller* the size of the hook. An average sized hook for most freshwater fishing would be between a #2 and a #12, with a #8 being a good choice. Once again, ask your tackle shop for guidance.

Hook sizes larger than #1 are designated with a /0 after them, as in 1/0, 2/0, 3/0, etc., all the way up to 12/0 (used for sharks and other huge species of fish). Occasionally, hooks of 1/0 to 4/0 are used for largemouth bass and other freshwater species, but these are specialty hooks, used with specific types of plastic baits, rubber worms, etc.

WHAT ABOUT LINE?

Line is designated by weight. That is to say that 4 lb. test line will break at approximately 4 lbs. of dead weight; 6 lb. test at 6 lbs., etc. Fish that are considerably heavier than the line weight being used can be caught with relative ease, by utilizing a combination of the bend in the rod (which acts as a shock absorber) and drag (which permits the fish to take line without breaking it).

Light freshwater fishing is generally done with 2-6 lb. class line; medium with 8-12 lb. test; and heavy with 14 lb. test and over. Saltwater ratings are proportionately heavier. Ask your tackle shop for recommendations regarding the type of fish you're after. Good line is NOT CHEAP, BUT it is the *CHEAPEST* part of your equipment. ALWAYS change line FREQUENTLY. Your LINE is the CONNECTION between YOU and the FISH. DON'T BUY CHEAP LINE!

SINKERS

Sinkers, or weights, are used to get your bait down to the fish. How much weight you use depends upon how deep the water is, and how much your bait weighs.

lead ball, varying in size and weight, which resembles the lead shot used in a shotgun shell. It is called a "split" shot, because of the jagged gash or "split" in its side. To put one of these on your line, simply lay the line in the "split" and squeeze the gash closed with a pair of pliers. DO NOT USE YOUR TEETH! (One of us has cracked the same tooth twice, resulting in expensive bonding to repair it as a result of using his teeth. What an idiot, huh?) DON'T USE YOUR TEETH! There, you've been warned.

A general rule of thumb is to use the least amount of weight necessary to get your bait down to the fish. Generally you want to position the split shot approximately 18" above the hook. Most tackle shops sell an assorted pack of split shots. That's what we recommend for most freshwater fishing.

There are other types of specialized sinkers, such as dipsey, rubber core, etc., and eventually you will probably try them all. But, we're sticking to KISS, remember?

For those of you who intend to try your hand in the salt, especially in the surf, there are two main types of sinkers used; pyramid and bank. These generally come in one-ounce increments, and which you use will depend upon the type of bottom over which you are fishing. Pyramid sinkers are used over sandy or muddy bottoms, because their pyramid shape permits them to dig into the bottom and hold their position. Bank sinkers are shaped like a large teardrop, and are used over rocky bottoms. Their shape keeps them from getting hung up in the rocks. The amount of weight will vary according to depth and current. The most common weights are one to four ounces.

FLOATS

Floats or bobbers (as they are commonly referred to) are used to either suspend bait at a particular depth, or in saltwater, to keep bait off the bottom and away from pests like crabs or skates.

The most common type of bobber used in freshwater fishing is the plastic type, usually round, ranging from ½" in diameter all the way up to the "Mongo" sized ones of 3" to 4" in diameter. They're usually brightly colored, with one half being red and the other white, or some other such combination. DO NOT USE "MONGO" ONES! One sure way to spot a beginner is to look for the guy or gal with a monstrous bobber attached to his or her line. Just like with weight, use the smallest bobber that will get the job done.

Attaching a standard bobber is quite easy. Just follow these steps:

1. Press down the button on top of the bobber. This will expose a little hook on the bottom of the bobber.

2. Pass your line under the little hook and release the button on the top of the bobber. This will retract the little hook back into the underside of the bobber, thereby trapping the line between and hook and the bobber.

3. Press down on the edge of the button on top of the bobber. This will expose a similar hook on the *top* of the bobber.

4. Pass the line beneath *that* hook, and release the button. The line will then be trapped beneath the hook and the button, thereby locking the bobber in place on your line.

You will be limited as to how far up the line you position the bobber by the length of the rod and how tall you are (try it and you'll see what we mean). If you are fishing in really deep water and wish to suspend your bait considerably farther down in the water, you'll have to use what's called a sliding or "slip" bobber. These come with complete instructions, so we'll not go into details at this time.

WHAT'S LEFT?

Other than hooks, line, sinkers, and bobbers, there are accessories called snap swivels, barrel swivels, and just plain snaps, all of which are designed to either aid in attaching various lures to the end of your line or to eliminate line twist, OR BOTH. Ask your tackle dealer for advice in purchasing these items. Sometimes it's not necessary to use them at all, especially if using bait.

A WORD ABOUT "LEADERS"

What's a leader? It is a piece of monofilament line or, in some cases, a piece of wire, attached to a hook, and then attached to your main fishing line. In most cases it is either lighter OR heavier than the main line being used. When a hook has a monofilament leader already attached to it, it is referred to as being a "snelled" hook. For most freshwater fishing, you do not need "snelled" hooks. Just buy a box of "unsnelled" hooks and you'll be all set.

When do you use a leader? Well, some instances might be when fishing for pike or pickerel in freshwater. These critters have very sharp teeth which might cut through your relatively light monofilament. In saltwater, you might use a steel leader to protect against the dentures of a barracuda or other toothy fish. ONLY USE A LEADER IF YOU ABSOLUTELY HAVE TO!

IN CONCLUSION

Well, as you probably realize by now, there are many terms, techniques, and items associated with fishing — even for a beginner — with which you must be familiar. We have only touched upon a few, but at least with this knowledge at your command you will be equipped to enter a tackle shop or approach a body of water without feeling totally naked.

CHAPTER 6

What Kind Of Bait Do We Use?

S ince we obviously wouldn't use the same bait in freshwater as we would in saltwater, let's separate the baits into the two categories, addressing the former first.

FRESHWATER BAITS

If you think all baits are created equal, think again! Not only are some baits more effective than others, but some are also more user-friendly than others, as well. For the purposes of this chapter, we will categorize baits as either "easy" or "yukkie." Let's start with "easy" and leave "yukkie" for last.

"EASY" BAITS

"Easy" baits can be defined as things you or your child can feel free to use without fear of getting "yuk" all over your hands. Your Little League star might not have any compunction about spitting on his mitts and wiping them in the home plate dirt, but hand him a wiggly worm and he or she just might make "yukkie" all over your hip boots.

KERNEL CORN: By far the easiest bait to use is kernel corn. Either yellow or white may be used, but most "experts" will generally choose yellow. NOTE: *Some states outlaw the use of kernel corn, so be sure to check with your local authorities before using it.* There is a widespread misconception that corn, when ingested by certain fish, especially those with small digestive tracts, i.e. trout, may block the stomach passageway, spoil, swell, and finally kill

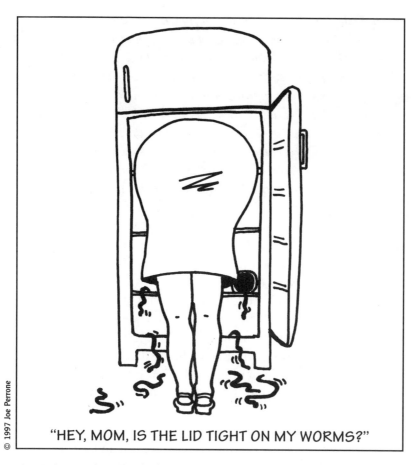

© 1997 Joe Perrone

"HEY, MOM, IS THE LID TIGHT ON MY WORMS?"

the fish. However, an experiment conducted by Tom Jeramasz, a long-time member of the fabled Knee Deep Club of Lake Hopatcong, New Jersey, appears to contradict the myth:

In the late 80's, Tom lived on the lake, and had a boat house, in which he kept his boat and fishing equipment. He also had a very large wire basket secured to the bottom of the lake (within his boat house) in approximately eight feet of water. The basket was about four feet square. One spring, Tom caught a handful of foot-long trout and placed them in the basket. Now, for sure, some small fish, insects, and other natural food organisms may have swum or fallen into the basket during that spring and summer, and became food for those trout. But, the principle food that the trout consumed was not "animal" or "mineral" as we used to refer to in that old children's game, but "vegetable," or, to be more specific, that Old Demon Corn!

Tom fed those trout canned yellow corn every day for quite a few months, and each and every one of those critters grew with the passage of time. Very few kernels remained on the bottom of the cage each day, so, clearly the trout had eaten the stuff and prospered. By the fall, not one of the fish had died; all were larger and Tom, having proved his point, released the happy and healthy trout back into the lake. So much for corn killing fish!

Another possible reason for people not wanting corn to be used as bait may be due to the fact that it's just *too good* a bait! The fish and game authorities may well feel that it kills fish, but more likely they have concluded that it is a "killer bait," and is just too effective. That would also explain why bait stores don't sell the stuff. After all, who would buy it from them, when they can get it at the "stupid" market for a third the price.

Corn as bait works clear across the land, just make sure you buy *kernel corn*, not the creamed stuff. You might possibly get away with it as chum, but try putting a mess of it on a hook — impossible!!

POWER BAIT — One of the more commonly used "easy" baits is "Power Bait" by Berkley. While other manufacturers produce similar concoctions, Berkley was the first to perfect this type of bait, and in fact, stands out in the field of artificial baits, much the way Kleenex outdistances the competition among makers of paper hankies, or Xerox does in reproducing documents.

The stuff comes in three basic forms: paste, nuggets, and artificial eggs. Each has its own advocates, but be assured, all of them work! Three elements account for "Power Bait's" success: smell, color and floatability. Probably the most important of these characteristics is SMELL (some insist it's floatability!) Each is produced by combining various ingredients (secret to be sure!), but it seems clear that whatever it is that is included must do a pretty good job of mimicking the food fed to fish in the various eries around the country. The concept is elementary — bind an odor into a bait that will smell irresistible to feeding fish — simple and effective! The smell is somewhat offensive, so resist the temptation to have junior inhale its aroma.

COLOR also seems to play a part in this bait's attraction, though no one person can agree as to which is the best. Some contend that fish are color blind. If so, why then are they attracted to one color one day and another the next? They may not be able to use semaphore code to communicate to each other with their fins, but they certainly can differentiate between colors. Pink often is best, but orange also does the trick. Today it may be chartreuse, and again, later in the day only white will do. Although manufacturers surely make the stuff in many colors partly to garner more shelf space, it is wise to carry several different hues just to be on the safe side. Consider one dark and one light shade as a matter of practicality.

One might ask, "FLOATABILITY? What does that have to do with anything?" Well, take a nugget, a blob of paste, or an egg, attach it to a hook, throw on a couple of split shot sinkers, two feet up the line and cast it into a body of water and you'll find out the answer. While the sinkers fall to the bottom, the "POWER BAIT" floats right up there, two feet off the bottom *where every fish in the area can SEE IT!!* Is it natural looking? Hell, no! But, who ever said fish are the rocket scientists of the animal world? They smell it, they figure out if it's the right color, but, most important of all, they can *see it,* right up there in watery space like a "fish cookie" being held out by its mother.

SMELL, COLOR, FLOATABILITY — Three reasons that make this type of bait good to use and not at all "yukkie" for a youngster to place on a hook. Remember, we're trying to catch fish, not turn the beginner's stomach inside out.

MARSHMALLOWS — Would you believe marshmallows as bait? Bet on it! We're talking the little "mini" jobs sold in bait shops. We can't swear the bottles of dyed ones we have seen are the same as we toast on a campfire, because they usually bear a warning like: "Not for human consumption." There is a distinct possibility that there may be flavor enhancers or attractants added which further induce fish to feed on them. At any rate, we have both used the grocery store variety and they too work just fine, thank you very much! The major problem with using the store-bought variety is that after your kid gets done wolfing them down, there usually aren't enough left with which to fish. So, remember the Perrone/Luftglass rule: "One bag for the kid, one for the fish!"

The fish most commonly caught by using marshmallows are trout, carp, chub, and catfish. White, or colored mini-marshmallows seem to work best, but don't rule out the use of full-size 'mallows for large carp. Imagine a large boil on the surface, the 'mallow being literally sucked down by the rubbery lips of a giant carp. Who knows, you might even have to grab the rod out of Junior's hands just to save him from fighting such a behemoth. Think of the kid, always the kid!

BREAD — No kidding! Bread makes a great bait for carp and catfish. We're not talking a slice here, Brainiac; just a small piece of bread kneaded into a ball and placed on the hook will most certainly attract every sunfish in the pond. Don't just limit your choice to Arnold's or Wonder white bread, either. Even a piece of floating poppy seed bagel can be effective at times. Pat Scaglione of Scag's Bait and Tackle in Staten Island, New York, tells us that he has customers who swear that the aforementioned bagel is the *preferred* bait for the large carp in the local lakes there. (NOTE: large carp are particularly difficult to fight and land for small children, so *do* be ready to take the rod if you suspect that such a fish has inhaled your kid's offering. We don't want any broken rods or crying children if we can help it.)

DOUGH BALLS — Probably the most commonly used "easy" bait is a simple dough ball. People have been fishing with this stuff forever! Not only does this simple concoction work on coarse fish, like shiners and carp, but a well-crafted dough ball has been known to take many a trout and even a salmon or two!

To make dough balls, simply take some plain white flour, add water, and whatever your heart desires for a scent. Some suggested aromas might include, but are not limited to: vanilla, anise, and maple syrup. Be sure to allow your child the pleasure of hand-crafting these little creations. Who knows, you might just be encouraging the next Paul Prudhomme. Common sense, combined with trial and error, will dictate just what consistency is best for fishing.

CORNMEAL BAIT — Basically a more sophisticated variation of the dough ball, cornmeal bait is a cooked product and is especially popular in English carp fishing, where the locals refer to the baits as "boilees," owing to the fact that the cornmeal balls are boiled after their preparation. The Brits boil yellow or white meal, flour, water, sugar, and a scent (some actually use chopped onion or garlic) to manufacture their "boilees." In Jewish households this is referred to as "mommah liggah," and in Italian homes it's called polenta.

CHEESE — As with marshmallows, caution must be exercised lest little Angela nibble all the goodies before the fish get a crack at it. Just take a chunk of white or yellow American cheese, or, our favorite, Velveeta, toss it into a Tupperware container, and you're ready to go fishing. All that's left to do is to mold a chunk around a hook and start casting. Be ready, this stuff works in lakes and ponds!

PEAS/BERRIES — Wherever there are mulberry trees with limbs hanging over the water, a single such berry attached to a hook is sure to entice a hungry carp to strike. A green pea affixed similarly will also yield equally-satisfying results.

SALMON EGGS — Although shore-bound anglers do not do as well with salmon eggs as those fishing in the moving variety of water (note: salmon naturally spawn — drop their eggs — in moving water), they still can be an effective bait. Properly used in a stream or river, salmon eggs are a top producer, with the usual prey being trout. Tributaries of the Great Lakes such as the famous Salmon River in Pulaski, New York, hold tremendous numbers of steelhead, brown trout, lake trout, and Chinook and Coho salmon which will eagerly vacuum a salmon egg from your hook if you are lucky. This is not fishing for beginners, and ought not be tried by any youngster who hasn't turned at least 13 years of age, *and* not without adult supervision.

SUPERMARKET SHRIMP — Sort of a crossover bait between "easy" and "yukkie," these morsels should be okay with even the most squeamish of youngsters. Peel one of these and you have a great bait, especially good for catfish.

"YUKKIE" BAITS

Here we literally separate the men from the boys. If you, "Mr. Grown-Up," do not like to handle "iggily, squiggily, wiggly" things, i.e. live critters, then forget this section and stick to "easy" baits. If, however, you are a full-fledged, breast-beating, hairy ape with loads of testosterone coursing through your veins, this part of the chapter is just what you ordered.

WORMS — First and foremost on the "yukkie" bait hit parade has to be the renowned worm. Depending upon availability, there are three basic kinds: garden worms, night crawlers (or night "walkers," depending upon where you live), and red wigglers or glass worms. The latter are extremely fragile, hence the nickname "glass" worm, but are also very active on the hook and extremely enticing to fish. They are found most often in leaf piles or compost heaps. Garden worms are just that — worms found in the garden. The night crawlers are the large earthworms with a band around the body which are found on your lawn at night after a heavy rainstorm. They make great bait for largemouth bass. Small pieces make good fodder for sunfish, perch, and other small critters.

NOTE FROM MANNY: *"Back in the fifties, my friend, Donnie Schildkraut, and I used to dig little red worms that had yellowish collars near their heads at Prospect Park in Brooklyn, New York. We would put fifty in a plastic container filled with wet peat moss, poke holes in each top with a hot needle, and stamped the tops with a yellow label. The label read "California Red Worms" — maybe we were off a little in our geography, but fish in Brooklyn liked our bait and we sold our 'product' to a bunch of stores, until the amount of effort exceeded the cash reward."*

Photo by J.B. Kasper

Pennsylvania resident, Jeremiah Kasper was eight when he caught this sunnie on yukkie bait.

LIVE SHRIMP — We ended the "easy" bait section with shrimp that you can buy in a super market, peel, and cut up — dead, of course. Now, it's time to deal with the *live* variety — grass shrimp. Not readily available everywhere, these little gems attract fish galore. Crappie, sunfish, perch, and pretty near every other commonly found freshwater fish will eat a grass shrimp. They do possess little stickers that can nail a delicate finger, so be careful when handling them.

LIVER AND MILTS — Catfish of every kind, striped and hybrid bass, trout, and other species all like this rather unattractive-looking bait. Milts (sorry, we don't know *where* the hell the name comes from) is nothing more than bovine pancreas. It comes from cows! Liver is liver — be it chicken or calf's. Both "milts" and liver definitely qualify as "yukkie," and usually require the availability of a wet towel — to wipe the "yuk" off of your hands, of course. Although we haven't seen "milts" lately in any local butcher shops (perhaps because of board of health concerns or some such technicality) it can sometimes be obtained in a Kosher butcher shop, and definitely makes a dynamite bait, and not just for catfish; trout love it too!

Liver is also a terrific bait and is less objectionable to youngsters, perhaps because it's not alive, and doesn't wiggle when being impaled upon a hook.

MEAL (BUTTER) WORMS — "Mealies," generally thought of exclusively as a trout bait, are actually not worms at all, but beetle larvae. But, call them what you will, they are great bait. In addition to trout, they are wonderful for pan fish, especially crappies.

LEECHES — Not just intended for curing blood ailments, leeches make terrific bait for smallmouth bass. Be sure to hook the first few for your youngster, being careful to show him the correct technique. They work very well, but are not for the faint of heart, as they are capable of squirming around and latching onto unsuspecting anglers' fingers.

CRAYFISH (*CRAWFISH* south of the Mason-Dixon line) — CAUTION: See LEECH above — Seriously, a crayfish can indeed turn around and nip a small finger, big time! So, here a little "show and tell" is in order. Remove the claws and you are on your way. A point of interest: crayfish molt, like lobsters, and, while in their unprotected, shell-less state are a particular delicacy for hungry smallmouth and largemouth bass, carp and almost any other freshwater fish.

HELGRAMMITES —These centipede-looking insects are actually the larvae of the dobson fly, a large flying insect which feeds on smaller flying insects. They are possessed of a particularly nasty pair of pincers, and can inflict a painful bite if not handled carefully. Not a bait for little ones to handle without supervision, but "Gawd" awful good as food for *large* trout, and large smallmouth bass.

LIVE BAIT — A category of bait that includes any small forage fish, i.e., minnow, shiner, alewife, herring, etc. These are generally fished alive and can attract some of the largest members of whatever species of fish you're after.

FROGS — Great bait for really large bass. Keep this one for yourself, or else you'll never get your kid to go see "Kermit the Frog" in a Muppet movie.

EELS — To you they may be eels, but to a child, they're more like e-e-e-e-e-e-l-s, because they are s-o-o-o-o-o l-o-n-n-n-n-g! Seriously, though, if you are going to use eels in rivers for striped bass, channel catfish, etc., keep them very cold, or wet your hands and dip them in sand, otherwise you'll have a hard time holding onto them. (Keeping them v-e-r-y cold reduces their natural slime layer, making them easier to handle.)

SPECIAL NOTE ABOUT "YUKKIE" BAITS: Be especially sensitive to the feelings of young children about using "live" bait such as minnows, killies, frogs, etc., because *all* youngsters are instinctively reluctant to kill living things, particularly small bait fish. Be sure to have a well thought-out explanation prepared for your youngster about predators and prey, and DON'T EVER FORCE A CHILD TO KILL A BAIT FISH, OR IMPALE ONE ON A HOOK IF HE OR SHE DOESN'T WANT TO DO SO.

NOTE FROM JOE: *"I remember taking my stepson, Jared, fishing for trout on the Beaverkill River in upstate New York; he was 13 years old at the time. I had hooked a brown trout deeply in the gills, and I knew from experience that it would probably not survive. I took the time to explain the situation to Jared, and told him that rather than letting the fish suffer, or be eaten by a predator, it was preferable to kill it and end its suffering. In spite of all my explaining, when I actually broke the fish's neck, Jared had an extremely negative reaction to the experience. To this day, much to my regret, except on rare occassions, he does not fish. Perhaps no amount of preparation could have prevented his discomfort, but even now, I wish I had done a better job of it."*

So, a word to the wise, "SHUT UP AND STICK THE HOOK IN!" is not a good enough explanation for even the most healthy-minded child. As a rule of thumb, it is best to stick to the "easy" baits until you're sure your youngster is old enough to accept the harsh reality of "live" bait fishing. Above all RESPECT YOUR CHILD'S FEELINGS, even if it means not getting beyond dough balls as the bait of choice.

SALTWATER BAIT

As in freshwater fishing, the baits of choice in the brine may be divided into "easy" and "yukkie;" your choices of "easy" are, however, a bit limited, we're afraid. In most cases, saltwater bait fishing requires handling "icky" if not "yukkie" bait, the latter being exponentially higher up on the "barf meter." (The barf meter is an imaginary measuring device which records one's response to handling unpleasant feeling or looking substances like raw clam or eels.)

EASY BAIT

CORN — Used as a chum for flounder, this easy bait acts more as an attractor than as actual bait.

DOUGH — A poor choice in saltwater is the little dough ball, however, it will take the occasional mullet and other small coarse fish.

Sorry to say, this brings us to the end of the "easy" bait section for saltwater fishing. But, good news, there are a number of "borderline" baits which rate fairly low on the "barf meter."

BORDERLINE BAITS

CLAMS — A top bait for nearly every fish that swims in the salt, they come in a variety of sizes and shapes including sea (skimmer), chowder, steamer, and little neck. Since they don't move or wiggle, they are usually not as repulsive to little ones as other forms of "live" bait might be.

SQUID — Undoubtedly one of the best baits for fluke, squid also attracts many other kinds of fish, including snapper blues,

Photo by J.B. Kasper

*This young lady was using a sandwich of a yellow soft plastic lure
and a squid strip when she caught this big ling.*

porgies, grunt and striped bass. Only the most squeamish will be
deterred from using squid, because it is neither slimy nor smelly.
Generally, mates on a party boat will be glad to clean and prepare
this bait for you. Be sure to have your youngster watch, so he or
she can learn the correct way of cutting this rather easy-to-use
bait. Squid can be bought frozen, or obtained fresh. Either way,
it is a great bait when cut into chunks or used in strips for fluke
and flounder.

DEAD FISH — This category is limitless, but can include such
favorites as butterfish, mullet, mackerel, herring, bunker, or even
such exotic species as ballyhoo. These baits are either fished
whole, or cut up into chunks, often to be drifted in a chum slick
(an oily paste of ground-up bait fish, ladled onto the surface of the

water, which acts like a smelly attractor.) Using whole fish is a good deal easier for a youngster, as it doesn't involve any cutting or filleting, which could result in messy fingers.

DEAD SHRIMP — Since we ended the "easy" bait portion of the freshwater section with these little gems, it's appropriate to end this saltwater section with them as well. The smaller shrimp that you can purchase in a super market are actually quite inexpensive, and we have caught more than a dozen species of fish when fishing from small boats in the north, and even more than that in Florida. Pier fishermen in Florida buy packages of frozen shrimp from tackle stores, and instead of fishing them whole, they peel and cut them into small pieces, which seem to give off more aroma. Your kid can gain instant credibility on the party boat circuit when he teaches his *secret* to some old salt who insists on fishing the shrimp whole in the shell. Guaranteed to increase one's catch!

YUKKIE BAIT

LIVE SHRIMP — Monster weakfish to the north and south all love to eat shrimp. Whether you use little grass shrimp or their bigger cousins, these creatures are great fish getters. We have examined the stomach contents of hundreds of fluke, and have found them loaded with grass shrimp. Bottom feeders in particular are extremely fond of this bait. What's not to like? After all, don't you love shrimp? Doesn't your kid? Just be careful of those sharp little spines.

LIVE FISH — Oh, boy, now we've got a problem! Maybe the child who likes to pull the wings off of flies might not mind this exercise, but many *will* be bothered by it. Prepare a good line of chatter to go with putting a live fish on the hook. You might try, "You know, Johnny, these are cold-blooded animals, and they don't have any pain sensors, so don't worry, they can't feel the hook." Or maybe you could use the old, "It's really nature's way, you know..." Whatever you do, look them straight in the eye and LIE! After all, isn't that what you'll have to do if you drop a still-struggling bluefish in the cooler? As far as what kind of fish to as live bait, the list is endless. Some favorites will surely include: mullet, bunker, sardines, killies (mummachog), and herring. Most important of all, be sure that the bait fish you use is legal where you are fishing. After all, we don't to teach Junior to be a criminal, just to fib a little.

EEEELS — No, those four E's aren't a "typo," it's just that the eels we use in saltwater are *that much longer* than their freshwater cousins. Use the same method for handling them that we previously discussed; that is, to roll them in sand, or keep them *really* cold. Nothing can beat a live eel for catching a striped bass.

CRABS — Fiddler or "China-back" used whole are wonderful, if you can find them. Green crabs used whole or with the top shell off and cut into chunks are also good, while in New England the crab of choice is the Hermit.

A live crab fished whole is the ultimate, but here we are faced with a dilemma. Who is going to get rid of those CLAWS? Show your child the proper way, or have the mate on the boat show both of you, so you can avoid being nipped by the little critters.

WORMS — Blood worms, sand worms, even yard-long tape worms all make G-R-E-A-T BAIT, but they all have one thing in common; they top the "barf meter" as YUKKIE! Some have pincers, others just wiggle a lot. Either way, you can watch a youngster turn a variety of colors as these creatures wriggle and squiggle on the end of a hook. Try these on land first to be sure your little one can tolerate the experience, before venturing out to the open sea.

Fishing with bait is actually far less dangerous than chucking lures with treble hooks. However, if your little one is *really* turned off by the slimy stuff, by all means, go to artificials. the important thing is that he or she is fishing *and* having fun! However, be prepared for less than spectacular results with the hardware, since bait will nearly always out-fish lures.

NOTE: *To quote Peter Wright once more (June 1994* Motor Boat & Sailing), "... *Action = Bait + Chum. The simple ABC of fishing!"*

CHAPTER 7

Can We Eat It?

C learly, if your children want to take fish home to eat, they will need to know the rights and wrongs about preparation. For that information, we suggest you consult a fish cook book.

The first time you take your youngster fishing — and maybe the next dozen times, too — he or she will surely want to bring the catch of the day home. Believe it or not, it will *definitely* happen! They may not necessarily want to bring the critter home to eat, but rather to display it to mom's delight, just like "show and tell" at school.

WHAT ABOUT "CATCH AND RELEASE?"

The merits of "catch and release" are many, from conserving a species to leaving some fish for the next guy to catch, but determining whether or not you and your youngster will practice the philosophy yourselves is a decision that should NOT be made on the water, but should be made ahead of time AT HOME! If "catch and release" is your cup of tea, DECIDE AHEAD OF TIME! Talk about it in the car on the way to the fishing hole. Make it clear to your child why you intend to let your catch go free. You cannot ask a wide-eyed youngster to become an instant conservationist at the exact moment that you are removing the hook from a fish.

Convince your five-year old son that a picture is sufficient "evidence" for the jury of his peers (*make sure you bring the camera!*). Then, when he is certain that his older sister will accept the photo as living proof of his new-found prowess with the rod and reel, you can be assured that the fast-swimming fish that you have just released will bring a smile to his face and *not* tears! So, now you've got a chance of creating a "catch and release" kid.

BRINGING HOME THE FISH

It matters not whether your youngster is a boy or girl when it comes to cleaning fish. Cleaning fish is a gender-neutral activity. The important thing here is to make it clear that "you keep it — you clean it!" You want your child to understand that bringing fish home is not only about showing off your trophy, but includes cleaning the catch as well. Case closed!

Naturally, you can't clean what's inedible, so be sure to have a cooler with plenty of ice on hand in which to transport your catch safely home. Fish is extremely delicate and particularly susceptible to spoilage, so get

© 1997 Joe Perrone

"MAYBE IT NEEDS <u>MORE</u> KETCHUP?"

it on ice as quickly as possible. Keep a separate cooler for your food and drinks — no explanation should be necessary here; this should be a "no brainer!"

If your child is too young to actually wield a knife and clean fish himself, be sure that he *at least* assists you in the cleaning process. Perhaps he can scale the fish (if it's necessary to do so) or just rinse out the cleaned cavities and dispose of the waste. If you already know how to clean fish properly, make sure you show your youngster just how to do it. You'll not only be teaching him a valuable skill, but will also undoubtedly be saving yourself a good deal of work down the road. *NOTE: Since there are plenty of books that both teach one how to clean and prepare fish to eat, we'll not deal with those subjects here.*

Suffice it to say that the question of "Can we eat it?" is far from a simple one to answer. Judging from our own experience, most children inevitably want to bring their fish home. However, once they are made aware of the ramifications of doing so, i.e. the necessity of killing and cleaning the fish, many youngsters will voluntarily opt to practice "catch and release." And, that's fine! Still others may not be deterred in the least by the processes involved in keeping the catch and that's okay, too! The important thing is to agree *beforehand* what will be done with the fish, *and* to make the youngster understand that the fish is NOT A PET! Oh, yes, that can happen, too!

NOTE FROM JOE: *"I remember when my youngest son, Matt, caught a sunfish and we brought it home in a bucketful of water. He insisted that we put it into the bathtub. Like an idiot, I gave in to his wishes. Well, everything was fine for a while, and we even managed to get the fish to eat a worm or two. The problem arose the following day, when, upon waking, we found the fish floating on its side, DEAD! It wasn't pretty watching a grown man tap dance his way to an explanation which involved everything from "Fish Heaven" to a discussion of chlorine poisoning and oxygen debt."*

So, as you can see, "Can we eat it?" can become "Should we eat it?" or even "Why should we eat it?" rather quickly. We want you to have a great fishing friendship with your child, so think carefully about this subject and be sure you *both* come to a meeting of the minds *before* a potential crisis develops.

We started off by kidding about "Do we have to eat it?" and have now turned the subject around to a serious discussion of conservation versus food for the table. Perhaps a good philosophy might be one that makes room for both points of view, just be sure that you *have* a philosophy that you *and* your child agree upon, *and* that you both stick to it. Remember, BE CONSISTENT!

CHAPTER 8

The First Experience

Fishing is more than just a hobby, it is a reflection of a philosophy of life. After all, in many respects fishing mirrors life, with its constant challenges, both in the public work place, and in our private lives. Each is filled with numerous successes and failures, but it is the manner in which we deal with these varied results that determines the kind of life we enjoy. Unlike real life, where failure often has dire consequences, fishing, in its most simplistic form, is a paradox whereby we are allowed to fail and yet still be successful. For it is the fishing that is the achievement, not the catching of the fish. There is satisfaction to be gained by merely *trying*. Teaching this philosophy to a child, however, is a horse of a different color. In the beginning, at least, a child *must* experience the feel of success that comes with *catching* a fish. Then, and *only* then, can he gradually begin to appreciate this "trying" thing.

If you make that initial foray into the world of fishing an unpleasant one, replete with mistakes and failures, the chances are good that your child will be a disciple of comic books, computer games, and the great indoors. But, do it *right* and you will have changed his or her life forever.

So, how do we insure a positive first time? How do we get it *right?* Believe it or not, it's actually quite easy.

FORMULA FOR SUCCESS

Before we actually go fishing, there are a number of things we

Photo by J.B. Kasper

Pennsylvania's Joshua Kasper was five years young
when his dad J.B. Kasper, well known guide and writer,
took this photo of Josh's first two trout!

can do in advance which will greatly enhance that first experience. For starters, take your youngster with you to pick out the tackle. As we mentioned in our chapter on tackle, if your child is under ten years old, the best equipment you can choose happens also to be the least expensive and simplest — a cane pole! That's right, just like Tom Sawyer and Huckleberry Finn used on the old Mississippi. The reasoning is that it is a sure fire piece of equipment — it's simple, has no moving parts, and can't possibly malfunction.

However, if your child is over the age of ten, follow the advice of the salesman (together with what you've hopefully learned from our chapter on tackle) and make your purchase. Listen carefully to what the tackle dealer has to say and you should come away with the right "goodies."

SIMPLE INSTRUCTION

Assuming that your youngster is old enough to be using a genuine rod and reel, and that you are experienced, you might start off by having him or her help in winding the line onto the reel. Most packages of line contain the necessary instructions for doing this, but just in case yours doesn't, here's how to do it:

Put a pencil through the holes in the spool of line, run the line through the guides (from the top) and attach the line to the reel spool with a clinch knot or a slip knot (also called an arbor knot — get a knot book if you have to!) and begin reeling. It's best if *you* hold the spool of line and let your child do the reeling. Be sure that the line goes onto the reel in the same direction as it is coming off from the spool. As your child reels the line onto the reel, make sure he maintains good tension, and that the reel is filled to within approximately one-eighth of an inch from the lip of the spool. Either secure the loose end to the little line clip generally found on the spool, or fasten it beneath a rubber band.

PRACTICE MAKES PERFECT

If you're smart (and we *know* you're smart because you bought this book!) you'll purchase a couple of practice plugs. These are brightly-colored plastic or rubber objects, designed to take the place of dangerous plugs, and they are used for casting practice. This is also a good opportunity to teach your child some basic knots (the knot book, remember?) Then, head out to the backyard or to the park and PRACTICE! This simple step will save lots of *aggravation* later on when you actually go fishing.

If your first trip is going to be in saltwater, you might want to show little Johnny how to release line (s-l-o-w-l-y, please) from a conventional reel. Explain the concept of backlash, and how it results from dropping the line without using the thumb to control the descent of the lure. Rig up a four or five-ounce sinker and have him start the release with rod tip held high, so he can observe the drop over a longer distance.

CREATE DESIRE

Another good idea is to take your offspring to the local "hot spot" and let him see others catching fish. Bring home fishing videos and watch them OVER and OVER. Don't suggest that he try it, but let *him* bring up the subject. Even then, be sneaky, say something like, "Oh, you don't want to do that, do you?" After all, you're the parent, you make the rules! Only after the kid has asked at least a half dozen times should you finally give in and take him fishing.

WHAT DO WE BRING?

The answer to this question is simple. You bring EVERY-THING BUT THE KITCHEN SINK! Seriously, the worst thing is to *not* have what you need for that initial expedition into the out-doors.

Aside from the proper tackle (which we've already discussed) the most important items you can bring are food and drink. Kids get v-e-r-y thirsty, especially if you are foolish enough to have left the drinks behind! Bring lots of liquids — preferably not sweet, syrupy drinks, or drinks with caffeine, since these will only serve to "hyperactivate" (is that a word?) your child and also attract ants, flies, yellow jackets, etc. Actually, ice water is probably the best libation, with natural fruit drinks a distant second. For snacks, good ones might include bananas, apples, grapes, pretzels, or even animal crackers — *if* your child is *really* young. Of course, if your youngster is a little older, you can probably skip the snacks and just bring a lunch — since this will probably be an all-day affair.

Next to food and drink, clothing is the most essential equipment we carry. Always bring a rain poncho, hat, and a sweater. If there's a way for your kid to get himself wet, he or she will find it, so pack extra shoes and socks; underwear; and a change of

*Delaware's Keith Kaufman had all the stuff needed
to keep his son Ross happy, including lollypops!*

pants and shirt. Include sunglasses (for the sun *and* as protection against errant hooks flying through the air), sun screen, insect repellent, band aids, needle-nosed pliers (for pinching down barbs and releasing fish), the *all-important* camera, and a pain reliever — for the headache you surely will encounter! Although it could sound a little gross, some might even include a "pee" pot and some toilet paper.

Since little ones do get bored easily, it might not be a bad idea to add a book or two, a puzzle, and even a ball or Frisbee for a game of catch. Remember, we *are* here to have *fun*. Stop-and-start fishing works real well for those attention-span challenged wee ones.

A good idea is to develop a checklist — and to use it! Be like the Boy Scouts and be prepared for every eventuality and you will have taken a major step toward having a successful outing.

WHAT *NOT* TO BRING

Just as it is important to *bring* the right things, it is equally important to *not* bring certain things. Above all, do not bring a buddy — either for your child *or* for yourself. There will be plenty of distractions without additional human appendages to take your mind off of your child. Leave any alcoholic beverages at home, as well as cigarettes, pipes, cigars, and other tobacco products. Kids are very impressionable.

Don't bring along profanity, impatience, or intolerance, either. These vices will only serve to ruin the day. Forget about radios, video games, and portable televisions. Not a good idea! Same goes for your cellular phone — if you *have* to bring it along (in case of an emergency) leave it in the car, where it belongs!

"STUFF"

In addition to the basic tackle, you'll also want the following additional "stuff:" a couple of coolers (one for bait and fish — the other for food and drink); a rag for wiping your hands; maybe a couple of folding chairs; a landing net — you may not need it to land the fish your little one catches, but it comes in mighty handy for scooping up minnows, frogs, and other such distractions your child might discover. A long-handled, fine mesh net is also helpful for catching live bait. Remember, this is junior's first time — anything goes! We just want to make it a *positive* experience — one that he or she will enjoy, guaranteed to insure a return engagement.

THE NIGHT BEFORE

Needless to say, *both* you and your child should get a good night's sleep before the big day. If you're planning on using dough balls or cornmeal bait, let the youngster make it himself, or at least assist you in the preparation. Also, have him lay out his clothes and check off the equipment that the two of you will be taking with you the next day. Try to end the evening with an activity that is *totally unrelated* to fishing — to avoid getting your child so excited that he or she can't drop off to dreamland. Above all, resist with all your might the temptation to set the alarm for four- thirty a.m. *Your* time will come soon enough — we promise!

THE BIG DAY

Once you are both up and around, make sure you each have a good breakfast, so you won't run out of fuel. Double check all your equipment, gather up your paraphernalia and head for the pond.

As you have probably realized by now, the hard part is over. Now comes the fun. Show your child how to bait up the hook, toss the line into the water and wait. If you've chosen the right place — God help you if you haven't — you shouldn't have to wait long. Pretty soon the bobber will disappear beneath the surface and Sonny Boy will yank out whatever creature has ingested his humble offering. Odds are it will be some sort of sunfish or other obliging creature in that distinguished family of fish. Take a picture of little Elmo with his prize, then carefully show him how to take the fish off the hook.

Be sure to release the fish gently so it will swim away unharmed, assuming, of course, that you and yours have had that little "catch and release" chat we recommended earlier in the book. If not, you can always say something like, "Oh, darn, I forgot to bring a cooler. Maybe we can keep one the next time we go fishing." Do this enough times, and junior will either get the idea or figure you out for the dirty, lying dog that you really are! On the other hand, if you have agreed beforehand to keep a couple of fish, just toss them into a cooler and continue fishing.

WHEN TO QUIT

If your kid is like most single-digit aged kids, he'll probably become bored somewhere around the half-hour mark — and that's fine. Stop fishing and perhaps just talk about what has happened so far. Now would also be a good time to eat that snack you brought with you. In addition, if you've brought one, maybe you can toss a ball around *or* go on the swings (most ponds like the ones we've recommended are usually located in a park that has swings and other diversions). If, after a little hiatus, your child doesn't ask to resume fishing, you may casually make such a suggestion. But, and this is IMPORTANT, under NO CIRCUM-STANCES should you FORCE THE ISSUE. When you've *both* agreed that you've had enough, *then* it's time to go home.

BACK TO THE RANCH

Once you've arrived home, it's time to tell fish stories. Let your child tell all about his or her big adventure. LET YOUR CHILD TELL THE STORY, *NOT* YOU! Never mind if he or she exag-gerates a bit — that's part of the fun. Don't encourage outright lies, of course, but fish tales are okay — in fact they are almost a ritual with *real* fishermen!

If you've elected to bring the catch home to eat, now's the time to clean it. Using good common sense, show your youngster the proper way to skin, fillet, or otherwise get the fish prepared for cooking. If your child is old enough and coordinated enough, perhaps you might let him try his hand at cleaning the fish as well. Cooking is next, and that is something that both boys and girls can be taught to enjoy.

NOTE FROM JOE: *"My first fishing experience came when I was about ten years old. We had moved to New Jersey from Brooklyn, New York, and my friends and I used to walk three blocks to fish in the Hackensack River in Oradell. At that time, the river was clean enough to support a population of stocked trout, but my usual catch consisted almost exclusively of sunnies and yellow perch, which I would bring home for my mother to prepare. I can still see her standing in our kitchen, apron wrapped around her waist, as she cleaned those fish. The best part of the ritual was when I got to roll the little fil-lets in flour in preparation for their being fried in hot oil. I don't know if those fish were particularly good to eat or not, but I do remember the feeling of importance I enjoyed as a result of providing my family with them. To this day I still enjoy the cooking and eating almost as much as the actual fishing."*

WHAT ABOUT NEXT TIME?

A part of American life that seems to have almost become an anachronism is the family dinner hour. A fish fry resulting from junior and dad's (or mom's) joint efforts is a wonderful opportunity to reestablish this tradition. It is a time for fish tales, and compliments for the fishermen and the cook. In short, it is just another positive way to cement the bonds of family, and to reinforce your child's confidence in himself. Usually it also serves as a stepping stone to the next outing, which can often be planned over dessert. Once again, it is important to let the child initiate the planning, if possible. While subtle prompting is fine, *never* pressure your child into committing himself to a "next time." Chances are, if you've done your homework, and followed the rules, your child will be chomping at the bit to go fishing again as soon as possible. And so it goes.

Chapter 9

Do's
And Don'ts

- ✔ **DO** TAKE A CHILD FISHING BECAUSE HE OR SHE *WANTS* TO GO — YOU'LL *NEVER* REGRET IT, AND YOU'LL PROBABLY HAVE A FISHING BUDDY FOR LIFE.
- ✘ **DON'T** TAKE A CHILD FISHING BECAUSE *YOU* WANT TO GO — YOU'LL *ALWAYS* REGRET IT, AND CHANCES ARE BEFORE LONG YOU'LL BE THE ONLY ONE FISHING!

- ✔ **DO** GET UP AT THREE O'CLOCK IN THE MORNING TO TAKE YOUR KID FISHING IF HE OR SHE *ASKS* YOU TO — EVEN THOUGH DAYBREAK ISN'T UNTIL SIX THIRTY.
- ✘ **DON'T** WAKE YOUR *CHILD* UP AT THREE O'CLOCK IN THE MORNING TO GO FISHING — AFTER ALL, WOULD YOU WANT YOUR KID TO WAKE *YOU* AT THREE A.M. TO WATCH CARTOONS?

- ✔ **DO** REWARD YOURSELF WITH A COUPLE OF BEERS WHEN YOU RETURN TO THE SANCTUARY OF YOUR HOME (AFTER FISHING WITH YOUR KID) — JUST *DON'T LET YOUR CHILD SEE YOU.*
- ✘ **DON'T** HAVE A COUPLE OF BEERS WHILE FISHING WITH YOUR YOUNGSTER — ABSOLUTELY, POSITIVELY NEVER — CHISEL IT IN STONE!

- ✔ **DO** ALLOW *YOURSELF* TO LOSE A FISH ONCE IN A WHILE JUST SO YOU SAY TO YOUR KID, "SEE, IT'S OKAY,

IT DOESN'T REALLY MATTER." OF COURSE, YOU CAN SOB QUIETLY ALONE WHEN YOU GET HOME.

✘ **DON'T** SMACK YOUR KID IN THE BACK OF THE HEAD IF HE OR SHE LOSES A FISH — *IT HURTS!* AND, BESIDES, PRETTY SOON YOU'LL ONLY HAVE YOURSELF AROUND TO KICK IN THE ASS, BECAUSE THE KID WILL BE *GONE!*

✔ **DO** TAKE A PICTURE OF *ANYTHING* YOUR CHILD CATCHES (EVEN A BOOT). NOTE: *BE SURE TO SHOW HIM THE OLD PRO TRICK OF HOW TO MAKE HIS FISH LOOK BIGGER. YOU KNOW, HOLD IT CLOSE TO THE CAMERA. (THIS MIGHT COME IN HANDY FOR YOU, TOO.) VALUES! THAT'S WHAT IT'S ALL ABOUT.*

✘ **DON'T** MAKE YOUR KID TAKE A PICTURE OF *YOU* HOLDING A FISH THAT *YOU* CAUGHT, UNLESS THE KID CAUGHT ONE, TOO — EVEN IF YOURS IS THE BIGGEST HYBRID BASS YOU'VE *EVER* CAUGHT!

✘ **DON'T** TAKE A PICTURE OF YOUR KID HOLDING A FISH THAT *YOU* CAUGHT, UNLESS YOU ACKNOWLEDGE THAT YOU CAUGHT IT. NO ONE WILL BELIEVE HIM, AND IT WILL BE NOTHING BUT EMPTY GRATIFICATION FOR YOUR CHILD.

✔ **DO** FORCE YOURSELF TO EAT *ANYTHING* YOUR CHILD CATCHES — WELL, OKAY, NOT *ANYTHING*, BUT ANY-THING *EDIBLE!* WARNING: JUST BE VERY CAREFUL *WHERE* YOU FISH AND USE LOTS OF KETCHUP!

✘ **DON'T** FORCE YOUR CHILD TO EAT A TROUT OR OTHER FISH THAT *YOU* CAUGHT IF HE DOESN'T WANT TO — EVEN THOUGH *YOU* THINK IT TASTES LIKE HEAVEN!

✔ **DO** BUY THE *BEST* EQUIPMENT YOU CAN REASONABLY AFFORD — ONCE YOUR CHILD DEMONSTRATES A *TRUE INTEREST* IN THE SPORT. GOOD EQUIPMENT CAN ONLY ENHANCE YOUR CHILD'S EXPERIENCE.

✘ **DON'T** BUY A LOT OF EXPENSIVE EQUIPMENT RIGHT

OFF THE BAT — YOUR KID WON'T KNOW HOW TO USE IT ANYWAY, AND BESIDES THE SALESMAN WILL SEE YOU COMING A MILE AWAY AND TRY TO SELL YOU THE PROVERBIAL STORE (AND YOU'LL PROBABLY BUY IT.)

✔ **DO** STAY AN EXTRA 15 MINUTES, OR, FOR THAT MATTER, AN EXTRA 15 HOURS — IF NECESSARY — IF YOUR LITTLE OFFSPRING *ASKS* YOU TO. BUT, *THE MINUTE* HE OR SHE LOSES INTEREST, GET MOVING HOME.

✘ **DON'T** EVER SAY TO YOUR KID, "JUST 15 MORE MINUTES, OKAY? I PROMISE, JUST 15 MORE MINUTES." YOU'LL JUST TEACH HIM WHAT IT MEANS TO BE A LIAR, AND BESIDES, HE'LL MAKE THAT 15 MINUTES THE MOST *MISERABLE* OF YOUR LIFE — WE PROMISE.

✔ **DO** FISH ALONGSIDE YOUR CHILD *ONCE* HE OR SHE HAS GOTTEN THE HANG OF THINGS; YOU CAN EVEN HAVE A LITTLE FRIENDLY *COMPETITION*.

✘ **DON'T** *EVER* FISH *YOURSELF* WHEN YOU'RE TRYING TO TEACH JUNIOR TO FISH. YOU CAN BE ASSURED THAT THE FIRST TIME HE GETS A TANGLE WILL BE WHEN *YOU* HAVE THE *BIGGEST FISH OF YOUR LIFE* ON THE LINE — AND, OF COURSE, YOU WON'T WANT TO QUIT TO HELP HIM UNTANGLE HIS "SILLY OLD KNOT." BET THE RANCH ON IT!

✔ **DO** INSIST THAT YOUR CHILD WEAR A LIFE PRESERVER *WHENEVER* THE TWO OF YOU ARE IN A BOAT. OH, AND DUMMY, YOU WEAR ONE, TOO!

✘ **DON'T** *EVER* LEAVE YOUR CHILD UNATTENDED FOR A MOMENT WHEN NEAR THE WATER.

✘ **DON'T** *EVER* PROMISE YOUR CHILD THAT HE OR SHE WILL *DEFINITELY* CATCH A FISH.

✔ **DO** BE PREPARED TO PUT ON S.C.U.B.A. EQUIPMENT —

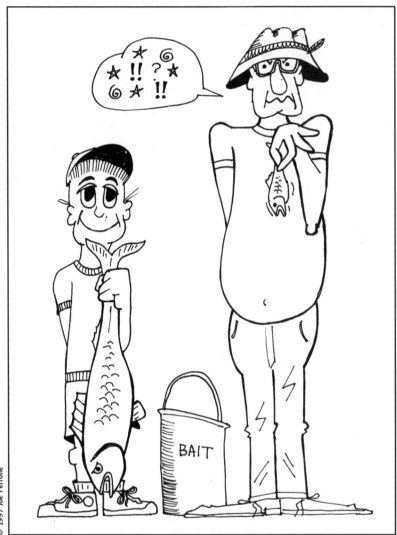

© 1997 Joe Perrone

IF NECESSARY — AND DIVE UNDERWATER TO ATTACH
A FISH TO HIS OR HER LINE IF YOU'RE STUPID ENOUGH
TO MAKE THAT PROMISE.

✔ **DO** *MAKE SURE* THAT THE KID DOES HAVE *FUN* —
EVEN IF YOU HAVE TO DO A CHEAP IMPRESSION OF
"BOZO THE CLOWN" TO ACHIEVE YOUR GOAL. EVEN-

TUALLY YOU'LL BE ABLE TO TAKE OFF THE MAKEUP AND BE YOURSELF.

✗ **DON'T** THINK FOR A MINUTE THAT TAKING A KID FISHING GUARANTEES THAT *YOU* ARE GOING TO HAVE FUN — IT'S THE *KID'S FUN* THAT COUNTS, REMEMBER?

✗ **DON'T** *EVER* TAKE MORE THAN *TWO* KIDS AT A TIME FISHING. *AND* IF YOU *DO* TAKE TWO KIDS FISHING DON'T FISH YOURSELF (IF YOU NEED AN EXPLANATION FOR THIS *CAVEAT*, PERHAPS YOU AREN'T A PARENT YET.)

✗ **DON'T** *EVER PROMISE* YOUR CHILD THAT YOU'LL TAKE HIM FISHING AND THEN *BREAK YOUR PROMISE*. YOU'LL *FOREVER* BE KNOWN AS THAT DIRTY @#*@#* OLD MAN!

NOTE: *In the June 1995 edition of* Sports & Field, *author Charles Gaines gives a lengthy list of Do's and Don'ts. His final admonishment bears repeating and can serve as a conclusion to this chapter: "DON'T GIVE UP, even if the first trip is a disaster. FISHING IS TOO IMPORTANT!" (We added the capital letters and exclamation point.)*

CHAPTER 10

Ice Fishing

Both of us grew up within the confines of New York City, where there weren't many places to ice fish, so neither of us really qualifies as an expert on the subject. In fact, each of would prefer to think of ice as belonging *in a drink*, rather than on *top* of the drink — with us standing *on* it!

Since many of you who are reading this book live below the Mason-Dixon Line — where there *also* is no ice fishing — we'll keep this chapter brief, in order to keep you from falling asleep.

"GRUMPY OLD MEN"

If, like most of us, you've seen one or both of the two movies featuring Jack Lemon and Walter Matthau as ice fishermen in Minnesota — competing on *and* off the ice — you probably view ice fishing as some sort of monastic practice better left to others.

It is our opinion that the two old geezers portrayed in the films were only grumpy because of the l-o-n-n-n-g winters that they were forced to endure in that northern state. Most residents of the colder climes find that ice fishing provides a welcome respite from winter's grip. Ice houses situated on frozen lakes offer a cozy place in which to continue fishing when the temperature drops below (and stays below) the freezing mark for months on end.

WILL A CHILD ENJOY IT?

Ice fishing can really be fun, both for you and your kids. The

Eight and nine pound northern pike caught in the open waters of Sodus Bay, N.Y. by Chris Schulz. This bay freezes like a brick in the winter and is great for ice fishing for pike.

finny critters that you'll catch will either be too small and/or too cold to put up much of a fight, so youngsters will be able to handle them with relative ease. Most important, is how you prepare for the event.

SAFETY FIRST

Right here we wish to be DEAD SERIOUS, because SAFETY on the ice is literally a matter of LIFE and DEATH. Put simply, the FIRST and ONLY rule you MUST OBEY is DON'T BE THE FIRST ONE ON THE ICE! Let someone else fish your favorite spot! Snow alone does NOT guarantee SAFE ice; often it may just serve to DISGUISE A THIN SURFACE — one that's UNSAFE for fishing.

PLEASE, PLEASE, PLEASE, don't be a big shot, ESPECIALLY if you have a child with you. The minimum thickness acceptable for SAFE ice fishing is SIX INCHES! Unless you are certain that there are at least six inches of ice on the lake, go bowling or to a movie. DON'T BE FOOLISH!

WHAT TO BRING

CLOTHING

Start off by dressing your child as if you were sending him out to build a snowman. Honestly, the requirements are basically the same for both activities. The difference is that you should really have darn near a full set of extra clothing for you and your child in the event that anyone should fall through the ice. You can consider the kid properly dressed if you have to give him a push to get him started walking.

Extra gloves are a must, too. You can make, book that your child will get at least one pair of them soaking wet — so, pack extra gloves, extra mittens, lots of them.

FOOD AND DRINK

Like anything else, you can't have too much of a good thing — like food and drink! Cold drinks are NOT a good idea; first because they'll lower your child's and your body temperature; second, because they are quickly converted to "flush stuff." Some good choices for beverages would be soup, hot chocolate, or decaffeinated tea.

Chances are that the "Cookie Monster" (from television's *Sesame Street)* was probably created on ice. Kids simply become ravenous on "hard water" because of all the activity. Oh, sure, *you* might just sit there on a bucket until you freeze solid, but a kid has no clue how to sit still. They'll constantly be on the move, making snow balls, snow angels, and the like. So, bring lots of "cookies" to feed the "Cookie Monster."

What about sandwiches? Sure, bring plenty! Peanut butter and jelly will do nicely — but it doesn't matter, just bring enough!

OTHER "STUFF"

This chapter is not intended to be a primer on ice fishing, but will hopefully offer another alternative to warm weather angling. If you are really into getting your child started ice fishing, be sure you are good at it yourself. Experimenting with a gas-powered ice auger while trying to supervise an energetic youngster is NOT something we recommend.

Ice fishing requires every bit as much attention as fishing in warm weather, so, if you bring more than one child with you, don't fish. You'll have plenty to do just keeping track of the little ones.

One piece of equipment that's proven invaluable is a sled. It's the best way to transport all your gear out onto the ice, as well as being a welcome diversion if your child becomes bored. Then, of course, there are snowballs to throw; snowmen to build; etc., etc., you get the picture!

Hey, there's only so much television a person can watch. So, if you and your kid have a terminal case of "cabin fever," try ice fishing. Who knows, you just might like it.

CHAPTER 11

"Ladies Day" And Other "Stuff"

A s a typical male reader, ask yourself this question: How many of you have ever seen a lady fishing alone with a child? We're serious! What... maybe two percent of you? Probably less! Having spent thousands of hours on various bodies of water, we two anglers can tell you, it just DOESN'T HAPPEN! Generally speaking, the only women we see fishing are those who are with someone of the opposite sex (usually someone BIG, who they swear is their husband, but is really their boyfriend.) A good rule of thumb is that the better looking *she* is, the more muscles and tattoos *he* has!

If you are a divorced mother reading this book, please listen carefully. If you are a man, perhaps an alimony-paying, ex-husband, yourself, listen *even closer*. Taking a kid fishing is a sure way of creating a positive aura about yourself. Others take one look at you and think, "Oh, what a nice person, taking the time to fish with his (her) kid." Get the picture? Ladies, go fishing alone with your kid, and somehow your rating on the "yummy meter" takes a giant tick upward.

Certainly there are those fellows who are out to catch fish, and only fish; they are the ones with the glazed expression in their eyes. They are usually "hooked" themselves. Leave 'em alone! But, then there are the men who are not "attached" who will see the great appeal in you, the woman fishing with her child — alone! You see, what he perceives is built-in fishing company — sort of a two-for-the-price-of-one deal — namely a glamorous lady with her ready-to-learn child. So, what does he get? Why, "hooked," of course!

So, ladies, don't listen to those folks who tell you to join a political club, a theater group, or a church/temple single parents club in order to meet the man of your dreams. Take it from us, if you want to find a man, TAKE YOUR KID FISHING!!

JUST PLAIN FUN

Okay, so you're not interested in all that "man hunting," sexist stuff; say you're a woman who just wants to have fun with her child. Well, fishing can provide that outlet, too. Bonding need not only be done at the shopping mall. Oh, sure, there's always lunch at a fast food restaurant; or sharing a bag of popcorn; or watching a little television together to fill that bill. But, take your kid fishing and watch what magic transpires.

A mom's relationship becomes far deeper and broader when she does something with her child that nobody else does with theirs. It's true! It sets her apart from all the rest of the mothers. Her child becomes especially proud of their unique relationship. Will they brag to their friends about their "special" mom? You bet they will!

Go fishing with your husband or boy friend, too, of course. But, if he is too busy, invite your child to come along. You'll both be better off for the experience.

MOTIVATION

There are many things that motivate kids, and we're sure you've tried them all. But, once kids are old enough to walk and talk — or so it seems — a major change occurs when they discover the value of money! Some of us start them off with "tooth fairy" money under the pillow, and others with "birthday dough," but suffice it to say, that sooner or later — usually sooner — your kid will discover the "almighty buck!"

How we treat this new-found awareness will determine whether or not we enhance our relationship with our new fishing partner, or, as often happens, goof it up big time! The outcome

*Derbies run by the Clinton Township, N.J.'s P.B.A. awards
EVERY kid with a prize. Here's Sgt. Mike Exley with son Brian,
along with Det. Dave Bye with son Dan, and their bluegills.*

depends *solely* upon how you go about it. So, listen and learn.

When we, as a parent, offer a cash reward directly to our child, it's as if we are bribing them. It's grossly insulting, and we urge you not to do it. There are plenty of places where a child can see that catching a big critter can mean dollars in the pocket. All you have to do is turn on the television and witness one of the many bass tournaments. Try to play down this idea though — kid's eyes will light up "TILT" quickly enough without your bringing it to their attention.

CONTESTS CAN BE GOOD

Fishing contests that are run by not-for-profit groups, like a Chamber of Commerce or a Lions Club, generally have a category for children — or are aimed entirely at the young folks, to begin with. This is a great way to get a kid motivated to fish with you. Trust us, a potential sack of cash will turn even the most disinterested youngster into a casting fool!

Often these types of organizations will offer a trophy instead of a cash prize, and that's fine, too. There isn't one among us who doesn't love to see our name emblazoned on a nice big piece of glittering hardware. How many of you still have your merit badges from the Boy Scouts, not to mention the numerous soft-ball, bowling or tennis trophies which adorn mantelpieces across the nation?

NOTE: *If you or your organization is interested in running a contest, it would be worth your while to refer to a story written by Gordon Holland in the March, 1990 edition of* National Parks and Recreation. *His article can serve as a primer for folks wanting to run a contest of their own (perhaps to benefit a charity, etc.). Pure fun is what Mr. Holland advocates, and in his story he tells how to prepare correctly for a fun-filled day for everyone!*

SOME EXAMPLES

One sure fire way to induce a youngster to try fishing is a party boat trip, with its allure of "easy money" to the pool winner as the brass ring.

NOTE FROM MANNY: *"More than twenty years ago, I took my daughter, Barbara, fishing with me on a head boat. Although she and her younger sister Sue had both been fishing with me in rowboats before, this time it was out to sea, and owing to dumb luck, everything worked out perfectly.*

"I had picked a half-day boat, 'the Norma K II,' from which to fish; it was out of Point Pleasant, New Jersey, and the summer flounder (fluke) were biting. Once again, 'Lady Luck' had shone her light upon us, because the weather was beautiful. A modest breeze helped move the boat on what was otherwise a calm ocean, and Barbara, using a little rod and closed-face Zebco reel, managed to hook and land a three-pound fluke. Her fish turned out to be the biggest of the trip, and she won the pool! I can still see her walking around the boat, carrying her fish and showing it to everyone as we headed back to the dock."

One's offspring need not win the pool, however, for a trip to be successful. Just competing for the jackpot often provides enough thrills to bring a youngster back to the water again.

NOTE FROM JOE: *"Several years ago, my stepson, Jared,*

Joe Perrone with step-son Jared Ruban, before Jared donned
Navy "blues." Appropriately, the fish are bluefish!

having enlisted in the Navy, was awaiting his entry. Since he
had never been on a boat before, I suggested we test his 'sea
legs' with a half-day bluefish trip aboard the 'Big Mohawk' out
of Belmar, New Jersey. The trip was fairly uneventful, that is
until Jared caught what appeared to be a potential pool-win-
ning blue. From that point on, his interest level jumped about
ten notches, as he alternately fished like a madman and ran
around the boat comparing the size of his fish to everyone
else's. It was nip and tuck down to the wire, until finally his

eight-pounder was just beaten by a fish that weighed about a quarter of a pound more. Jared received a ticket good for a discount on his next trip as a consolation prize and couldn't have been prouder if he had won a new sports car — I didn't have the heart to tell him that those discount coupons were customarily given to everyone on a party boat."

Sometimes, it not only pays to be lucky; it pays to have a creative relative as well.

NOTE FROM MANNY: *"My step children, too, have experienced the lure of winning pool money, having shared a few pools themselves. But, one day in particular stands out which illustrates how prizes need not be given in dollars to effectively induce youngsters to fish with their parent.*

"Jen and Henry were about ages five and seven, respectively, when Suzan and I took them to a fishing contest held at a local pond, and sponsored by a neighborhood club. We figured it would be good for them to catch some fish, and maybe win a prize or two.

"As things developed, Jen caught the first fish by a girl, and even the biggest, thereby netting herself a prize. Although Henry also caught a fair number of fish, there were many more boys than girls entered, and his entries didn't land him a trophy. Well, not quite! He ended up with a memento bearing the inscription: 'Most Fish By a Boy,' or something like that.

"Of course, there was no such trophy, but not wanting him to be disappointed, his 'creative' relative had secretly ordered a bogus trophy, which I picked up along with the real one which had been won by Jennie. Shhhh, don't tell him."

Bribing kids to go fishing is not a very good idea, but friendly competition with a prize or two at stake — well, why not?

CHAPTER 12

Grandchildren
(Your Last Chance)

I f (like one of us) you failed to make a go of fishing with *your* child, and you think it's too late to make amends, relax. There's always the role of the grandparent. As a grandparent, you are entitled to certain rights and privileges, among which is the right to take your grandchildren anywhere you choose.

*"Gramps" Manny, on right, with son-in-law, Greg Morea,
along with grandchildren Joseph and Rebecca.*

Grandparents are viewed by little people as saviors — saving them from "Do this!" and "Do that!" and "Do it now!" The challenge to you, as a grandparent, is to resist spoiling them — at least while their parents are watching!

It is hard to imagine a grandparent or grandchild not bonding well with one another. Oh sure, you could goof it up if you are as rough on them as you were on their mom or dad, but, most of us tend to develop more patience as we age, and this should be a major advantage in dealing with our more distant offspring. Naturally, if you follow the advice we have given to you in the preceding chapters, you'll almost certainly be up to the task.

A grandchild who asks, "Can you take me fishing, Gramps?" has you by the proverbial "short hairs," and knows it! Of course, they may have to share you with a sibling, or a friend who tags along, but they *know* they've got you hooked. Sort of reminds us of the young man who chases the maiden until *she* catches *him*!

In addition to the joy of fishing with a young person who loves being in your company, there is another possibility which probably has not even crossed your mind — a second chance to fish with *your own child!*

This is the perfect opportunity to invite your son or daughter along on the trip. After all, can't you just hear your grandchild imploring his parent, "Come on, dad, it'll be fun!" And, believe it or not, it *will be!* Hell, you've read the book! You know what to do! What are you waiting for? It's your last chance — go for it!

Glossary

(Everything You Need To Know About Fishing And Then Some)

alewife n. 1. a small N. American bait fish, resembling a herring *2. a beer- drinking spouse*

anchor n. 1. a heavy object, usually made of metal, lowered from a boat by line and chain, to prevent drifting *2. an undesirable mate (sometimes referred to as a "ball and chain")*

angle v. 1. to fish with a hook and line *2. to use tricks to get something (to angle for a prize)* **angler n.** *one who inserts lead weights inside a fish in order to win the pool*

bait n. 1. food or other substance put on a hook to attract a fish *2. v., to torment or harass, verbally or otherwise, i.e. call into question another's angling skills — **bait and switch**, offer one thing and deliver another, e.g. (see **lure**)*

barb n. 1. a sharp point projecting to the rear of the main point of a fish hook *2.v. a smart-aleck remark often made by a spouse regarding a fisherman's lack of prowess (most often on fishless days)*

barf v. 1. to vomit *2. n., what you vomit; (usually the sinker (see **sinker**) you ate for breakfast)*

barf meter n. *1. imaginary device for measuring the potential for barfing based upon the condition of the seas, the type of bait being*

*As for "Catch & Release," eight year old Matthew Perrone
(Joe's son) couldn't wait to release this big bass.*

*used, and how many beers and/or sinkers (see **sinker**) you have
ingested*

bass n. pl. bass 1. a spiny-finned food or game fish in fresh or
saltwater 2. ***bas' the mumbled first syllable of a frequently-used
expletive, i.e. "...get your hands off that fish, you dirty bas'..."***

bass boat n. 1. a boat used for bass fishing 2. *an over-priced,
over-powered, outrageously-outfitted, floating, finished basement,
used by rednecks for storing and consuming enormous quantities of
beer; occasionally used to fish from*

bobber n. 1. a device, made of cork, wood or plastic, used to suspend a bait above the bottom of a body of water; also called a float *2. redneck pronunciation of the name for one who cuts your hair*

cast v. 1. the act of tossing a bait or lure into the water 2. *n. an ensemble of fishermen pooled together to verify the untruths of another, i.e. cast of characters*

catch and release v. 1. practice of deliberately releasing a caught fish for purposes of conservation and sportsmanship *2. the unintentional release of a potential trophy; usually caused by careless playing of the fish (sometimes referred to as* **long-distance release***)*

chum n. 1. a paste made of ground up fish, used as an attractant 2. v. the act of spreading the attractant upon the water with a ladle *3. n. a beer-drinking associate of questionable repute, usually overweight*

conservation n. 1. official care and protection of natural resources *2. protecting one's last cold beer from other fishermen*

current n. 1. a flow of water in a definite direction *2. happening now; recent, e.g. "...he has the most* **current** *bass lure — the Maxi Magnum Manipulator*

drag n. 1. a device on a reel, usually consisting of a series of washers, designed to provide resistance to a fish taking line, thereby slowing its run and tiring it *2. what a trip on an all day party boat can be with a five-year old, especially in foul weather*

fish n. 1. any member of a group of cold-blooded animals which live in water; has a backbone, gills for breathing, and fins *2. an easy mark or dupe, e.g. "...that fish will buy any bass lure advertised on T.V.: 1. v. to catch or try to catch a fish (more often than not, the latter)*

float n. 1. (see **bobber**) *2. what you hope you'll do when the wake of a speeding bass boat tosses you into the water*

guide (s) n. 1. the circular projections attached to a rod (see **rod**) which help to steer the line through to the tip top (see **tip top**) 2. a knowledgeable individual who acts as a paid assistant to a fisherman *3. this book!*

head n. 1. a slang naval expression used to describe a shipboard toilet *2. the part of your anatomy that you'll wish you had left at home after spending a day on a head boat in bad weather (see **head boat**)*

head boat n. 1. a slang expression for a party boat *2. description of a party boat in rough water, since most occupants spend the trip in the **head** (see above)*

hook n. 1. a curved piece of metal with a point, used to catch fish *2. v., to catch by a hook — by hook or by crook, by any means, honest or dishonest; in fishing, often the latter*

leader n. 1. the end piece of fishing line attached to the hook or lure, usually of a lighter or heavier gauge than the rest of the contents of the spool *2. a redneck term **lead'er** used to direct a fish into a net, e.g., "...**lead'er** in thar, boy!"*

line n. 1. the material (usually monofilament nylon, braided nylon or braided Dacron) which serves as the connection between the fisherman and the fish *(not to be mistaken for "string" which is what divorcees, novices and rednecks call **line**) 2. what fishermen are often accused of giving their wives after a day's fishing 3. v. act of telling a falsehood related to fishing, e.g., "...don't you just know he's **line**"*

line test n. 1. the amount of dead weight required to break fishing line, e.g. four-pound test will break at approximately four pounds + -, unless it is IFGA (International Fish and Game Association) rated, in which case it must break at four pounds or less *2. an intensive interrogation given to a youngster to determine whether or not he or she is* **line** *(not telling the truth) about a specific fishing occurrence (used often by jealous fathers); also used by suspicious wives*

lure n. 1. (see **plug**) *2. something that tempts or entices, often in a misleading fashion, e.g. a good-looking, member of the opposite sex*

pan fish n. 1. small freshwater fish, usually sunfish or perch, easily cooked in a frying pan *2. the part of the fish that sticks to the bottom of the frying pan*

party boat n. 1. a commercial fishing boat, available for hire to the general public, which charges each patron a set fee (see **head boat**) *2. just what it sounds like!*

perch n. 1. a small, spiny finned, freshwater food fish *2. a similar, bony saltwater species 3. a fixed spot, usually in a precarious location on a boat or on shore, from which most anglers manage to fall*

plug n. 1. an artificial lure, usually made of wood or plastic, designed to imitate a bait fish *2. an endorsement for a particular product, usually made by some redneck on a "made for T.V." bass fishing show 3. v., to fish incessantly in the same spot, regardless of the potential for success (done often by those having imbibed considerable alcoholic beverages)*

pole n. 1. a slang expression for a fishing rod 2. a fishing rod used by a redneck *3. a person of Polish descent (who may or may not fish)*

reel n. 1. a device with a spool, upon which line is stored, used for fishing 2. v. to wind on a reel *3. to stumble blindly across the* *deck of a head boat, usually after consuming a second six-pack of beer*

release v. 1. to let go, e.g. let a fish go; often done intentionally (see **catch and release**) *2. n. a six-pack or two of beer taken medicinally, after unintentional catch and release of trophy fish*

retrieve v. 1. the act of winding line (see **line**) back onto the reel (see **reel**) *2. to get back; recover, e.g. to retrieve one's self respect after being out fished by a five-year old child; very common*

rod n. 1. a long, tapered instrument, usually of graphite or fiberglass, having numerous guides and a tip top used for fishing *2. what you would like to use on your kid when he insists on landing your fish!*

school n. 1. a group of fish, all of the same species, and generally of similar size *2. the least likely place to find a child once he has discovered fishing*

sinker n. 1. a lead weight used to get bait to the proper level *2. a donut or other baked good, usually eaten hurriedly before a party boat trip, which lays heavily in one's stomach; often disposed of involuntarily in the head (see **head**)*

tackle n. 1. equipment; gear — ***terminal tackle*** — *equipment, gear sold by fishing widow at garage sale*

tip top n. 1. the end of a fishing rod *2. the final guide at the end of the rod 3. condition of an individual after fishing with his kid!*